Evert Van der Hart

Sermons by the Late Rev. Evert Van der Hart of Rochester, N.Y.

With Introductory Sketch of the Author

Evert Van der Hart

Sermons by the Late Rev. Evert Van der Hart of Rochester, N.Y.
With Introductory Sketch of the Author

ISBN/EAN: 9783337160272

Printed in Europe, USA, Canada, Australia, Japan

Cover: Foto ©Lupo / pixelio.de

More available books at **www.hansebooks.com**

The late Rev. Evert Van der Hart

―OF―

ROCHESTER, N. Y.,

―WITH―

Introductory Sketch of the Author

―BY―

Rev. E. Winter, D. D.,

OF

GRAND RAPIDS, MICH.

A. Van Dort, Printer,
GRAND RAPIDS,
1890.

Rev. Evert Van der Mart.

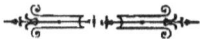

To the various Churches, over which during his life the author had been settled as pastor, this little

Memorial Volume of Sermons

Is gratefully and prayerfully inscribed by the widow of the beloved dead.

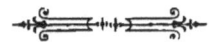

Introductory Sketch.

IT is with melancholy pleasure, that the writer undertakes to draw a brief sketch of the life and labors of one, whom he loved so well, and whose death—which seems to us all too early—he most sincerely mourns. But as there are no mistakes in Providence, we are to bow in silence,.assured, that even this early removal of an earnest worker from the Church on earth will serve some holy and gracious purpose * * * *

Evert Van der Hart was born on the 28th of January, 1847, at Nykerk, in the Province of Gelderland, and Kingdom of the Netherlands. In 1856 his parents came to America and settled at Pella, Marion County, Iowa.

Early in life, there were already unmistakable evidences of pious attachment to the Saviour and his cause. In this the Lord showed to his pious and praying parents, that He was faithful to his Covenant promises, and that their prayers were answered. Nor did the observing and interested eye of his beloved pastor— the Reverend P. J. Oggel, afterwards Professor at Hope College —fail to notice in young Van der Hart such traits of character and such evidence of mental power, as gave promise of usefulness, if only a suitable education could be had. His parents were unable to bear the burden of expense connected with a higher training. Other ways and means were now devised to secure the needed education. By the efforts and at the advice of the pastor, the younger portion of the Church, already named, the means were pledged. The Church did not fail to make its promise good.

After some preparatory studies at Pella, he was sent to Hope College, Holland, Mich.,—from which he graduated in 1869.

His theological course was also taken at Holland.

In 1872 he graduated. Shortly afterwards he was licensed, ordained and installed as pastor over the Second Reformed Church of Grand Haven, by the Classis of Grand River. This occurred on the........of April, 1873.

During the ministerial life, that followed, results fully proved, that the project, conceived by the pastor of the 1st Reformed Church of Pella, was wise. Nor has that Church ever had cause to regret the pecuniary sacrifices made for the object in view, even though at that time the expense was very considerable. That Church could point to Rev. E. Van der Hart with loving pride as her son in more than one sence, and had, and still has, reason to bless the Lord for whatever of sacrifice she made for his training for the sacred ministry.

True, sometimes there appeared discouraging signs. There was a time, at least, when, apparently with good reason, grave fears were entertained, that bodily weakness would blast all hope of future service. But the Lord's hand at last removed all reasonable ground for apprehension.

It was at the time, when those ominous signs seemed most discouraging, that the writer of this sketch became his pastor, and was brought into such close relationship with him, that an intimacy began, which lasted until death removed him from earthly fellowship. Through intimate acquaintance and the most confidential fellowship, the writer became most firmly convinced of young Van der Hart's earnestness of spirit, and his holy ambition to fit himself for the pulpit. The many questions asked, the conversations drawn out, the books perused, the models looked at—and, in addition, his zeal in study, and his prayers—*all* these pointed to the pulpit and the ministry, as the goal for all his energies and life.

And that he attained to a remarkable degree of proficiency in preaching—in unfolding the riches of the Gospel—will hardly be called in question by those most competent to judge.

These very sermons, bound up in this volume, will give at least some evidence on this point.

Of cource, he had his weaknesses and imperfections, as well

as all others. Constitutionally nervous and self-distrustful, he was at times unduly given to despondency. The heavens seemed dark, and all around he saw discouragement. This often made him appear at great disadvantage; nor was he then correctly understood by all. Such anxieties did he suffer at times from this cause, that his most trusted friends could scarcely cheer him up. But ordinarily these seasons were but brief. Faith and prayer would conquer and make him conquer. Thereby he would in due time emerge from his gloom—and rise above clouds and obstacles real or imaginary—above fears and anxieties.

Ardently devoted to his Master, to his cause and word, he was bound up in his work. That engaged all his attention. With an intentness of application, that is born of loving devotion and enlightened conscientiousness, his heart and soul and life were all consecrated to his Master's service.

In his preaching he was earnest and faithful—orthodox and yet free from narrowness—evangelical, but not afraid of referring to Sinai; as a pastor he was painstaking and sympathetic. As such he endeared himself to his people—both in the Presbyterian Church and in the Reformed.

People everywhere will cling to a pastor, who can feel for and with them, particularly in the days of sorrow and bereavement. In that school of sorrow and bereavement, he had learned the secret and the worth of christian sympathy.

During his first pastorate at Grand Haven, the Lord sorely afflicted him by calling his beloved and loving wife suddenly to Himself. He was left a griefstricken widower, the father of a little son, whom his youthful companion had left in his care.

At the end of four years, he took charge of the Reformed Church at Battle Creek. But all efforts to keep that Church alive were futile. It was in moribund condition. He might figure as sexton, chorister and organist and preacher—as he did —but all of no avail.

Happily, his former Church at Grand Haven was quite anxious that he should return. They extended a call—which was accepted. During this second pastorate, which lasted two years, he was married to Miss Jennie Brouwer, of the same place, who now as widow mourns the loss of her husband, and the father of her babe, only four months old at his death.

* * * * * * * * * *

From Grand Haven, at the expiration of this second pastorate, he moved to Mason, Mich., and became pastor of the Presbyterian Church at that place. This pastorate lasted but one year and six months. Ill-health now compelled him to take a long vacation. This was another trial, which left its mark upon him, but no doubt proved a spiritual blessing. As soon as he had sufficiently recovered to assume a charge, the Presbyterian Church at Albion, Mich., extended a call, which was accepted. Here he labored for two years, during which the Church had the misfortune of losing its house of worship by fire—but during which time also that Church was blessed in unusual manner. At the expiration of these two years of successful labor, the newly organized Church at Jackson, Mich., extended an urgent invitation to him to assume the work of building up that youthful, but promising enterprise. Here he labored hard for three years. In addition to the pastoral work, he had here on his hands the task of erecting a house of worship. The anxieties and labors connected with the mere oversight are enough to wear one out. But the work was happily completed and the congregation rejoiced in the possession of a commodius house of worship and a beloved pastor.

Another field of labor, however, was now ready. There had been organized at Rochester, N. Y., a Second Reformed Church —consisting of young, or Americanized Hollanders. The English language was to be adopted in all church services. That Church now invited Bro. Van der Hart to assume the pastorate. His experience in the Presbyterian Church had fitted him admirably for just such a field. The selection was a happy one. The call was accepted, after earnest deliberation and prayer. Brother Van der Hart, though leaving his beloved flock at Jackson and the Presbyterian Church with reluctance and heartfelt pain, entered nevertheless upon his work at Rochester with full decision, an earnest purpose, and bright anticipations.

But here the ways of God cross our paths, and cut short our expectations. Suddenly—on Monday morning, while the harness was still on, just two years to date after his arrival at Rochester, the Lord called him to rest from earthly labors, and enter upon the joys and services in the Heavenly Temple. This sudden removal not only made a beloved wife a widow and two children fatherless, but also filled a shepherdless flock with unfeigned sorrow. And elsewhere, all around, it awakened sorrow and sympathy. The funeral services held at Rochester were not only largely attended, but were most tender and touching. And among the many gratifying notices and messages of condolence sent to the mourning widow and son, there was a communication from the pastors of the Presbyterian Union of Rochester, which gave touching proof of the affection borne to, and the esteem cherished for, the deceased during life.

Not the Church at Rochester alone, but all others over which he had been settled, were warmly attached to him. And in every field the Lord had owned and crowned his labors.

It was his lot to become successively the first pastor of three Churches. And his was the unenviable task of having the oversight of the erection of three Church edifices. Not these edifices, however, but the influence exerted—the souls blessed thereby for eternity, are his monuments. Though his ministry was comparatively brief, it had been owned and blessed of God. And his memory is cherished with a true affection, and with gratitude to God.

As one evidence thereof the request has been repeatedly expressed, that a volume of memorial discourses might be published. As his sermons were nearly all in English, and some most deeply interested friends would be unable to read sermons in Dutch, it was deemed best to publish the sermons in English.

Of course, they had not been prepared for publication. Though the author himself might have made changes, if he had prepared them for publication, the writer of this sketch has contented himself with only such changes as were necessary. And in the selection reference has been had chiefly to the wishes that have been expressed.

The last two discourses were preached the day before his death. They are therefore placed at the close. Our only hope and prayer is, that this unpretentious volume may be attended with a Divine blessing—and may prove a welcome memorial to many of a pastor they loved in life, and cannot forget while he is dead. In these discourses, "though dead, he yet speaketh."

E. WINTER.

Grand Rapids, Aug. 26, '90.

Not Ashamed of the Gospel of Christ.

> For I am not ashamed of the Gospel of Christ: for it is the power of God unto salvation to every one that believeth, to the Jew first and also to the Greek. ROM. 1:16.

THE apostle tells his Roman brethren, in the verses which immediately precede our text, how anxious he was to see their city, and how he had once and again purposed to visit them. This fervent desire to see Rome was perfectly natural in a man of the apostle's taste and intelligence.

Nothing had made such a bold figure in history as this imperial city. From a small village, it had in the course of a few years, become the mistress of the nations, the grand metropolis of the world.

The mere name of Rome was already sufficient to awaken curiosity. But it was not the vastness of its extent, not the grandeur of its colossal structures, not the pride of its world-renowned institutions, not its peculiar laws and customs, that made him pant to enter its gates.

Nay, he longed to see Rome, not for any mere selfish interest; not in order to gratify his natural curiosity, and to admire human art and wisdom. But the great object he had in view was to impart to the beloved and called of God, within the walls of this vast city, *some spiritual benefit.*

Paul wanted to see Rome, in order that he might raise the banner of the cross in the midst of the emblazoned battlements of this proud city. He knew what vast multitudes were still groping here in Heathen darkness. He knew how many with all this external promp and splendour were daily perishing. He knew how unsatisfactory and transitory were "the lust of the eye, the lust of the flesh and the pride of life" which the masses were pursuing. And therefore he eagerly longed to offer them something which was real and enduring. Nor was he ignorant of how much this readiness and promptitude to preach the Gospel even at Rome would cost him. He was well aware, that there was no earthly inducement for him to go there. On the contrary, when he looked at his own interest, there was every reason for him to stay away from this wordly city—for there is a certain degree of shame attached to the Gospel, which the apostle preached. But, in view of all Jewish prejudices, and Gentile pride and every thing which makes the Gospel accursed in the sight of men, Paul boldly exclaims "I am not ashamed of the Gospel of Christ."

In this assertion, the fact is implied, that the apostle *might have been* ashamed of the Gospel. Let us therefore inquire

I. Why He Might Have Been Ashamed Of It.

He might have blushed, when he thought,

1. OF THE GOSPEL ITSELF.

What was this Gospel which the apostle preached? The term Gospel is an obsolete English word—from *Goodspell*—meaning "good news."

Now, the *preaching* of the Gospel is simply the announcement of "glad tidings"—the announcement of the happiest news, that can be communicated to a lost and perishing world. The Gospel tells us, that perfect happiness is attainable. That man can be delivered from sin and its awful consequences, and enjoy the most intimate fellowship with his God. That he may share in the glory and bliss of the angels in heaven. That his thirsting soul may drink of the water of life, which proceeds out of the throne of God. That he may aspire to a happiness, which "eye hath not seen, nor ear heard, neither hath entered into the heart of man."

Is there anything in this to be ashamed of? Nay, it is not so much the salvation itself, but more especially the *condition* upon which it is obtained, that wounds human pride. The Gospel, which Paul proclaimed—taught, that these unmeasured weights of bliss and glory, might be reached simply by faith in the righteousness, atonement, and intercession of Jesus Christ,—a man, who was cast out by his own countrymen, and died as a malefactor amid extreme agony on the accursed cross.

It taught, moreover, that for this Jesus of Nazareth, men must leave their all, deny themselves, and take up their cross. It promised them, that if they should part with everything, which they naturally loved, and to which they clung, and put their entire trust in him, and could devote themselves wholly to his service—they would receive at once full and free salvation. Now what can be more offensive, than such strange, seemingly inharmonious teachings. How could the Apostle call this "GOOD-NEWS!" What could it effect? It only called out repugnance and enmity. To the Jews, it was a stumbling-block, and to the Greeks it seemed foolishness. That man could be saved, not by observing the law, not by leading a moral life, not by offering "thousands of rams, or ten thousands of rivers of oil; not by giving his first-born, for his transgression, the fruit of his body, for the sin of his soul," but simply by trusting in the life and work of a person, whose earthly career had terminated in such an inglorious, ignominious death—what could be more repulsive to the man of this world—than the teaching of such doctrines!

They seemed to be foolish, illogical, unintellectual, unphilosophical, absurd. To hold up to the enlightened world such seemingly contradictory doctrines—might have been considered the very height of folly. What wonder, that such a one should expose himself to all manner of shame and ridicule.

2. Again, the Apostle was liable to have become ashamed of the Gospel, when he thought *of himself*.

What a splendid education had he received? Had he not been one of Gamaliel's most promising pupils? Had he not been trained in all Jewish customs and habits. Had he not for many years been a strict Pharisee, who ought to work out his salvation through the observance of the law? It must have been no easy matter for him, to count all those things, which had been gain to him, as infinite loss for Christ, and to cast away forever his own righteousness, in order that he might be clothed with the righteousness, which is of God by faith. When he thought of his *teachers*, his *companions*, and *friends*, when he looked back upon his past career, there was even reason why he should stand abashed.

His *intellectual ability*, too, might have kept him back from such strict adherence to the Gospel.

Paul was by no means an ordinary man. He was well versed in all the wisdom of his age. His mind had been thoroughly disciplined. He was a reasoner, a philosopher, a thinker. Not without reason did Festus say to him—"much learning doth make thee mad." He might have taken his place among the most brilliant minds of his age—but, on account of the bold position he took with respect to the Gospel of Christ, he excluded himself from their ranks—and was greeted by them as a vain babbler. Surely, it demanded no little faith in the Gospel, and no small degree of self-denial, to stand unmoved amid the countless sneers and taunts, which the apostle received from friends and foes. It manifested a most wonderful firmness, and decision of character in the apostle—that he could look in the face of the many wise, the many mighty, and the many noble of his time, and say "I am not ashamed of the Gospel."

3. Once more, he might have been ashamed of the Gospel, *when he thought of Rome*. This city was, at this time, the mistress of the world. Here riches, pomp and glory alone were held in great admiration. Here was found the height of genius and learning, united to the grossest profligacy of manners. Here the humbling doctrines of a religion, which demanded such severe self-denial, would naturally be scorned and derided. All these things might have restrained the apostle from going there to preach the Gospel. But nothing could do this. He does not even hesitate for one moment—" For he was not ashamed of the Gospel"—no matter how illogical and foolish it might seem to the haughty Roman. He had stood firm at Jerusalem where the whole strength of Jewish ritualism rose against it; at Athens, where it was confronted by the power of Grecian wisdom; at Ephesus, where the dazzling subteties of heathen magic rose against it; at Corinth, where the torrent of human lust and

pleasure rushed against it. Nor would it quail at Rome, where the concentrated energy of earthly idolatry would rise up against it in battle-array. He was not ashamed of the Gospel of Christ, though all that was intellectual and eloquent, and sensual and refined and powerful in humanity should protest against, it or mark it as folly.

It is very evident, that the apostle must have had some wellfounded reason why—in view of so much which might lead him to shame and confusion—he stands with a bold, unflinching countenance.

Let us, therefore, secondly inquire

II. Why He Was Not Ashamed Of The Gospel.

He gives the reason for this in our text " for it is the power of God unto salvation to every one that believeth."

I The Gospel was by no means the weak and childish thing, which men said it was. Had this been so, he would have been ashamed of it. But it was mighty—mightier than all philosophy, argument or eloquence. It was a *power*, a *vast*, a *boundless power*.

The apostle knew how much this Gospel had effected. He knew how much it had done in his case, and in the case of many others.

He recalled to mind so many, whose lives had formerly been a disgrace, but who had now become ornaments of society, " jewels in the Savior's crown." He was not blind to the marvellous changes which the Gospel was producing every day in hearts, in families, and in communities.

Nothing than this blessed Gospel could bring about such marked changes—which so affected all the different phases of society.

When he thought of so many trophies of the Gospel—of its astonishing results—during the few years, that it had been proclaimed, and of the victories it daily achieved over the world, satan, and the corrupt passions, and habits of the human heart, he could not refrain from calling it a *power*, and more than this, a *power of God*. This expression power of God does not convey. as some think, in accordance with an assumed Hebrew idiom, the idea of *great* power, which is often the case in Bible language, but it teaches us, that the Gospel is the grand means through which God exercises his power.

The Almighty manifests his power in all the works of his hands. He speaks, and it is done—but nowhere is his power more gloriously displayed, than in the Gospel of his Son. The Gospel in itself—as well as those, who proclaim it—is weak and seems foolishness. But in it omnipotence is wrapped up and God himself makes it mighty to the conversion of souls.

Nowhere in all the wide Universe do we find such wonderful power, directed to such a glorious end.

Marvellous is that divine power, which has scattered the stars, these shining orbs, like dust along the firmament, and holds them in their courses; adorable is that power, which has watched over us and guided us from our sleeping infancy to this present hour. But what is this power, manifested in our preservation, when compared with the power, which raises us from our state of degradation and sin, to the inestimable privilege of sons and daughters of God. What omnipotence it demands to break those hellish chains, with which the sinner is enslaved, and to make him a possessor of the liberty of the sons of God.

This power does not fail to acomplish the end it has in view. It is unto *salvation*. It delivers man from sin and condemnation, and restores him to the favor and fellowship of his God. It restores in us the image of our Creator, and makes us meet for the inheritance of the saints in light. Salvation! It is that, which no means of man's devising, no efforts of human wisdom or human power could effect for any human being. In vain has the wisdom of men, during the four thousand years, which preceded the advent of Christ, sought to discover adequate means, by which this most needed blessing could be obtained. The wise, the noble, and the great, have left men in the dark.

No Jewish observances, no Grecian culture, no Roman greatness, could give a satisfactory answer to the all-important question, which arises at some time or other in every heart "What must I do to be saved?" The Gospel alone meets man's great necessity as a lost being. It tells him how he can be saved. It is itself the power of God unto salvation.

Who can tell what this single Gospel has accomplished. No mortal can begin to enumerate the blessings, which it has bestowed upon us. It has changed the whole face of the world.

What dark clouds it has dispelled. How many a desert has it caused to rejoice, and to blossom as the rose. How many a traveller has it sent off on his desert way rejoicing. How many a one it has enabled to cut off his offending hand, and to pull out his lusting eye.

How many a one it has helped to make a full surrender of himself to the will and service of his Lord. Through the influence and power of this Gospel, men have rejoiced amid tribulation, and even raised their voices in song in the midst of the consuming flames. The mighty power of this Gospel cannot be estimated; there is no end to it. It achieves miracle after miracle. It overcomes the world. It does not quail before all the powers of hell combined. It is on this account, that the great apostle of the gentiles is not ashamed of it. Had it been less than this, however intellectual, and philosophical, he would have been ashamed of it. No other excellence, however great, however appreciated by the human intellect, could compensate for the want of this.

2. The apostle was not ashamed to preach the gospel of Christ even to those, who were at Rome—because they were with all their worldly advantages equally devoid of happiness, and needed salvation as much, as the most unenlightened Barbarians. Besides, the Gospel was as much for them as for any other nation under the sun—" for the grace of God, that bringeth salvation, hath appeared to all men." This message of good news is as wide as the world; it embraces all kindreds, and nations and tongues. It goes first to the Jew; it begins according to the divine arrangement at Jerusalem; but it does not end there. It travels all around the earth; it takes in all men, the Greek as well as the Jew—Barbarian Scythian, bond and free. And whosoever receives it, finds it to be a mighty power, and obtains from it a real and lasting benefit. In view of this, had the apos-

tle no reason to exclaim "I am not ashamed of the Gospel of Christ?"

3. Another attractive feature of this Gospel was *the simplicity of its conditions*. Its requirements were not high, to which but few could attain—but they were such, that nobody needed to be excluded from enjoying the salvation, which it offers. "It is the power of God unto salvation to *every one that believeth*." That is the condition. It does not ask of us something, which we cannot do, or which requires such exertion, that we might well shrink back from it—but its only condition, or better, the key, which unlocks all the riches of salvation to us, is faith, a firm, abiding trust in Jesus Christ as offered in the Gospel.

Now there is no one, who may not exercise this faith.

Every one, therefore, whether he be poor or rich, bond or free, ignorant or learned, may become a participant of this glorious salvation. The gospel brings good tidings of great joy, which shall be to all people. Well might the apostle, therefore, exclaim —even in the face of all scorn and opposition "I am not ashamed of it."

But it is very evident, that the apostle means to convey more than these words at the first glance seem to express.

He does not merely want to tell us—that he is not ashamed of the Gospel—but by a rhetorical figure, by which a thing is represented as being less than it really is—he means to say, that he glories in it, as he does in nothing else. That he counts all things as dross in comparison to its excellency. That he had determined not to know anything, save Jesus Christ and Him crucified. It is, as if he said, as he does to the church of Galatia "God forbid that I should glory, save in the cross of Jesus Christ."

It is but another way for expressing his firm confidence and fervent love for the Gospel. Would to God that every disciple of Jesus could say with the same depth of feeling, and with the same determination of heart "I am not ashamed of it." Were this the case, we would see the Gospel make still greater progress through the length and breadth of the earth, than it does to-day. For most glorious are the effects of this not being ashamed of the Gospel of Christ.

Let us briefly notice

III. The Effects of This Upon The Apostle.

1. It made him *an earnest preacher of the Gospel.*

As soon as he himself had felt its wonderful saving power, it became his fervent desire to proclaim these glad tidings of salvation through Jesus of Nazareth to others. No wordly considerations, no earthly comforts, could keep him from pursuing a work demanding such vast sacrifices. He knew by personal experience what infinite value the Gospel had, and how it answered to the one overwhelming necessity of perishing men. In view of this, he felt what great responsibility rested upon him. He therefore called himself in this chapter a debtor both to the Greeks, and to the Barbarians; both to the wise and to the unwise. Oh! what a debt the apostle did have. Every day he labored enthusiastically to cancel a part of that vast, enormous debt, which he owed to the world, and to his blessed Redeemer. His anxious desire was to publish the glad news of salvation,—no only where men had already heard of Christ, but he loved to go according to the divine command into the hedges and highways, and to invite all the maimed, the halt, and the blind to the great Gospel feast. With the speed of one, who knows that there are but twelve hours in a day, and that the night soon comes, in which no man can work, he hastens from city to city to speak of God's good-will to men. In this great work he allowed himself no rest, but pushed it forward with accelerating zeal, till he closed his eyes in the embrace of death thus showing in very deed, that he was not ashamed of the Gospel of Christ.

2. But he not only manifested this by his *earnestness*—but also by his *boldness as a preacher.*

Paul was bold as a lion—nothing could restrain him from preaching the Gospel in its fulness and simplicity. He did not mind the snares of the Jews nor the hostile influence of the Gentiles. He did not care whether the Jew called it a stumbling-block—or the Greek looked upon it as foolishness, because he was fully pursuaded, that "it was the power of God unto salvation. On this account, he proceeded courageously from one city to another, although the Holy Ghost told him, that bonds and afflictions awaited him. No bloody stripes, no damp pestilential prison walls, no torturing rack, or consuming flames could for one moment silence his lips. Without fear or confusion, he appeared before kings and judges—and rejoiced, that he was counted worthy to suffer shame for the name of his Master. Who can estimate, what this earnestness and boldness of the apostle has accomplished.

How many dark places of the earth has he caused to rejoice in the light of truth. How many Heathen temples he demolished. How many walls of partition he tore down. How many lost sheep he restored to the great Shepherd's fold. He was the means of leading countless hosts from the road to perdition on the narrow path, which leads to the Paradise above. Could they all speak to-day, how many voices would we hear around the throne, how many on earth, all thanking God, that the apostle had not been ashamed of the Gospel of Christ. Voices too, coming from Rome, for Paul's desire to visit this city was at length gratified. He saw this famous city—but not perhaps as he had expected, for God's thoughts are above our thoughts, and His ways above our ways. He entered it in the character of a prisoner, driven thither by persecution; and after being shipwrecked upon a certain island. There, in his own hired house, he preached the Gospel for two years to all that came in unto him,—and here in this proud metropolis, as everywhere else, it proved to be the power of God unto salvation.

Paul had the great satisfaction to leave some footprints behind him in this city also. And the brethren at Rome learned not only from his letter to them, but they saw with their own eyes, that he was NEVER and NOWHERE ashamed of the Gospel of Christ.

At the end of two years of faithful labor at Rome, he was set at liberty. As in former years, he laboured zealously to advance his Master's cause. During the cruel reign of Nero, he fell once more in the hands of his enemies, and was brought back to Rome the second time. No such mild treatment awaited him this time, as he had formerly experienced. All alone he lay in the dark, chilly dungeon. After a second trial, he was condemned and taken to the place of execution three miles from the city, where he, after a solemn preparation, cheerfully gave his neck to the fatal stroke—and verified, what he long before this had declared, that "he was ready not only to be bound, but also to die, for the name of the Lord Jesus."

My Christian friends, would to God, that the mantle of this great apostle and faithful disciple of Jesus might fall on us all. But alas! nothing is more evident, than *that there are many, many disciples, too, who are ashamed of the gospel of Christ*. They may not show this, when they meet with their fellow disciples,—but they manifest very sadly a spirit of shyness and backwardness, when they come in contact with the enemies of the Gospel. Many may not be ashamed to bear the name of a Christian, but they are ashamed to stand firmly by the principles of Christianity. Some look upon the Gospel to-day as something, that has served its time, and which must now give place to something higher, and more in harmony with the "deep instincts of humanity." Others consider it bare and unintellectual, and would overlay it with the gold of philosophy and eloquence to make it more respectable and attractive to the natural heart, which is enmity to God.

My friends, what are all such attempts to take from it or add to it, but proofs, that men are ashamed of it? There is in our day a peculiar tendency to bring the Gospel down to the common level of human wisdom, to reconcile it with the wisdom of this world, so that it may no longer be a stumbling-block to the Jew and foolishness to the Greek. But how little does this Gospel, remodeled after the style of our vain ages, accomplish. It is utterly powerless. It leaves the heart cold. It does not break the chains of sin. It cannot bring salvation nigh.

What the world needs to-day is Christians, who, like the apostle Paul, shall stand up before the whole world—and who in view of the great progress of science and philosophy—in view of all the learning and culture of this age, shall declare with a bold countenance, and without quivering lips "I am not ashamed of the Gospel of Christ." The world more than ever needs men, who by their words and lives, bear evidence, that they love the old apostolic Gospel, which alone is a power of God unto salvation.

The reason, why so many lack this firm stand for the Gospel, is because they have not that faith in it, which Paul had. They have not experienced its mighty power to save.

Ah! did they know the glorious salvation which it brings, they would not be ashamed of it, but it would be the only object of their glorying, and the endless song of their life. Ah! my friends, the redeemed in heaven, who have experienced its power and seen its glory, are not ashamed of it. The angels, who were its first heralds are not ashamed of it. God, who is its author, is not ashamed of it. Why should we poor sinners be? Why should we be ashamed of the greatest boon of heaven—of that, which brings us SURE, IMMEDIATE, ETERNAL SALVATION. To be ashamed of it, is an unmistakable evidence, that it has not done for us, what it *can do*, and *ought* to do—that we are not *saved*.

If this is the case, it has come to us in vain. It is not sufficient, that it reforms, elevates, and refines. If it has only made you moral, or kept you moral, it has sadly fallen short of its blessed end. Oh, dying sinner, remember it is the power of God unto salvation; the arm that lifts you up to heaven.

And that power becomes manifest in us, the moment we believe. A Gospel not believed, will do nothing for us but condemn. Have you welcomed the Gospel with its saving influence to your heart, or is the evil heart of unbelief still shutting it out? Is it still appealing to you in vain?

Is it still telling to you the old story of the love of God, the love of Christ, but telling it in vain? Have you not yet discovered the Good News, which it brings to you?

To-day if you hear his voice harden not your heart.

The Heavenly Mustard-seed.

Another parable put he forth unto them, saying, The kingdom of heaven is like to a grain of mustard-seed, which a man took and sowed in his field:
Which indeed is the least of all seeds, but when it is grown, it is the greatest among herbs, and becometh a tree, so that the fowls of the air come and lodge in the branches thereof.
Math. 13:32.

BEFORE us lies one of those beautiful, life-like paintings, with which the sermons of our Lord ever sparkled.

It shows us what lessons and illustrations may be gathered by the observing mind from the simplest things in nature. This parable is one of seven, which are strung together like glittering beads upon a silken thread. Each one glistens with its own peculiar luster. From the parable of the Sower, in which three-fourths of the scattered grain perishes, and was non-productive; and from the parable of the Tares, in which other formidable hindrances come to light, the disciples might be tempted to lose heart in spiritual husbandry. A brighter and more inspiring picture is, therefore, held up to them in the parable before us.

Our Lord here compares the origin, growth and development of his kingdom to the gradual unfolding of a vegetable seed. We are rather surprised, that he compares the expansion of his eternal empire to that of the trivial mustard seed. We would have rather expected, that he would have compared it with the stately cedar of Lebanon, or to the luxuriant growth of the Eshcol vine. But he selects this for a purpose. By this imagery he designs, not merely to set forth the ultimate greatness of his kingdom, but also its lovely origin.

For this end he could find nothing so appropriate as the mustard seed, which was proverbial among the Jews for its littleness, and yet reached an amazing height in those warmer climes. We are told, that in Judea and other hot countries this plant will sometimes grow to such dimensions, that a man can climb up into its branches or ride on horseback under them.

Besides, this vegetable plant was not as worthless in the eyes of the ancients as we might suppose. It was favorably known for its medicinal virtues against the bites of venomous creatures and against poisons, and was used as a remedy in many diseases.

Its fiery seeds were a great luxury to the fowls of the air, which, when it was ripening, would light in great numbers on its boughs. and build their nests under its screening foliage.

Beneath these vivid word-paintings, the most impressive lessons lie hidden. We are here emphatically taught what glorious developments in the kingdom of heaven spring from the slightest and most despised beginnings.

While in the histories of all earthly empires the general course is from the greater to the least, in the kingdom of heaven, which Jesus came to establish, the fundamental law is—from the least to the greatest. All the great schemes of this world look very promising at the outset. Like towers of Babel, their splendid fabrics loom toward heaven, but speedily they end in a deserted, and formless heap of rubbish.

Not so the kingdom of our Redeemer. It has an unobserved, and most unpretentious beginning, and by a gradual increase attains a most glorious consummation. This is true, whether we look at its founder, or at its process as it manifests itself in the individual heart or in the world at large.

Our Savior was born in a stable, cradled in a manger, raised and educated in an obscure Galilean village.

His surroundings were all of the humblest nature. For many

years he toiled at the carpenter's bench, cheerfully aiding in the support of Joseph's family.

When he began to preach, the prejudices of his country-men were aroused, because they knew the humble stock from which he sprang, and the little schooling he had enjoyed. Destitute of all earthly celebrity and power, the great and learned stood aloof from him. A few fishermen and publicans, drawn by the magic of his person and teaching, had the courage to enlist in his cause.

For two or three brief years, he preached in the towns and villages of Galilee, and occasionally at Jerusalem. Here and there an impression was made, and a few believed in him as the Christ. But his life terminated most suddenly, as well as most ingloriously, as judged by wordly standards. Under a cloud of night he allowed himself to be captured without the slightest self-defense, he was scourged and mocked and finally nailed to the accursed cross, where he died between two murderers, amid the greatest agonies. Such is in brief the history of the founder of Christianity. But as the tiny mustard-seed, when cast into the garden plot, gradually swells and bursts into organic life, so did the Christ of history. In him those words, which he uttered before his death, were most literally fulfilled—" Except a corn of wheat fall into the ground and die, it abideth alone; but if it die, it bringeth forth much fruit."—His death was the perpetuation of his life; his humiliation the manifestation of his glory.

He, who perished as a malefactor, is now crowned with immortal honor, and bears a name, which is above every name. Before the portrait, which the four Evangelists have painted of him, men of every age stand in rapt admiration.

At the feet of this once despised Nazarene, the great and noble of the earth to-day prostrate themselves, and lay their costliest treasure.

The growth from the least to the greatest, as illustrated in the growth of the mustard seed, is also true in the development of spiritual life in the individual heart. Could we know the first and almost imperceptible beginnings of those illustrious Christian lives, whose names stand out most prominently in the history of the Church, and whose influence is still a living power in the world, we would stand utterly amazed. A few single Gospel truths, uttered by a stammering tongue, fall upon the ears of a godless man. They sink into his heart. They arouse his conscience from its dormant state. They create new fears, new desires, new love, new aspirations. They change his entire inward life, and outward conduct. Old things pass away, behold, all things become new. As the mighty rivers, upon whose banks large cities leap into existence, and upon whose bosoms floats the commerce of nations, have their origin in some little mountain spring, so the most powerful and useful christian lives may be traced back to some little incident, some earnest word of exhortation, or some kindly act. A word of faith in the power of Israel's prophet, which dropped from the lips of the little Hebrew captive maiden, led to the marvellous cure of Naaman, and made the great Syrian warrior an earnest worshipper of the true God.

The preaching of Paul to that little group of Jewish women on the banks of the Strymon, resulted in the conversion of Lydia, and turned her home into the first missionary chapel on European soil. A kind invitation, given by childhood's lips, brought the restless and almost unmanageable Dwight L. Moody to the Sabbath school, and to-day his praise is in all the churches.

A few strains of a Christian song led a confirmed infidel to serious thought and prayer and he, who was once a bold propagator of infidelity, is now one of the foremost Evangelists upon the continent of Europe.

We might multiply illustrations.

But we must hasten, and call your attention to the principle of our text, as set forth *in the growth of the Church as a whole.*

How small and powerless was that little band of disciples, who, for fear of the Jews, had met with closed doors, upon the first day of Easter. The world would have smiled at the thought, that these few timid men would found a universal kingdom, that would grow in power and grandeur, amid all the changes and upheavals of the ages. Yet, what has history proved? Scarcely fifty days have rolled by since the propagator of this new religion died a most inglorious death, and behold, five thousand receive the seal of discipleship in one solitary day. Almost every day the cause of Christianity received a fresh impetus. The once trembling, but now heroic, inculcators go from place to place and cannot be silenced by the fiercest threats, and the most shameful abuses.

Persecutions, the most shocking, cannot arrest her, but only enlarge her boundaries and increase her influence.

Within three centuries, she has mounted the throne of the Cæsars, and, with the royal purple on her shoulder and the royal diadem on her brow, she gave laws from the very throne, before which she had been dragged as a criminal and condemned as a malefactor.

Then came those dark mediæval times, when the candle of divine truth was hid under a bushel, and the Church thought more of costly cathedrals and gorgeous vestments and empty ceremonies, than of true spiritual culture and missionary efforts. But after these days of Egyptian darkness, the era of the reformation dawned, which gave a new impulse to Christianity, whose healthful life is still beating in the pulse of the Church.

We hear it occasionally said by some of the enemies of our holy religion, that the Church is waning. That it is smitten with a blasting mildew, that its leaves are shrivelling, and its branches are dying.

Not long ago, a "non-church goer," came out in a popular monthly, and made the marvellous statement, that the Church was rapidly on the decline, that in "these days, only a small proportion of the intelligent and eminently respectable people are regular attendants upon religious services on Sunday." How people will dare to make such bold statements about things, which they have not taken the least pains to investigate, is most astonishing. The fact is, my friends, that the Church, instead of losing ground, never grew more rapidly. Dr. Ward, whose connection with ecclesiastical literature and the religious press is such, that he has every facility for looking into this subject, gives some encouraging statistics, which ought forever to put a stop to such false statements.

There is in the United States a population of fifty millions of people of all ages. Of these over ten millions—more than one in five—are communicants—not nominal members or adherents, but actual communicants—in Evangelical Protestant Churches. "We are within bounds," says Dr. Ward, if we say, that these represent thirty millions of people, who recognize themselves as attendants or adherents of the Church. The greatest majority, then, of our American people are frequenters and supporters of the Protestant sanctuaries.

But to these, according to the best computations, must be added some six millions of Catholics. This leaves us, then, according to the lowest estimates, some fourteen millions, which are not in the habit of attending the sanctuary.

But are these the best elements of our American society? Who will dare affirm this? Are these 800,000 habitual drunkards, who go reeling through our streets; are these 505,000 priests, who serve at the altar of Bacchus; are these countless wives and children, who suffer pauperism and brutality at the hands of their intoxicated husbands and fathers, all attendants on religious services? If we subtract from these fourteen millions the saloon and grogshop population, together with the inmates of our prisons, hospitals and poorhouses, it leaves a very small margin indeed for "the eminently respectable people," outside the Church.

But we have not yet begun to show you the progress made by the Christian church during this present century. We live in a country, whose growth in population, as well as in material resources, is a marvel in the history of any people. It is said, that during the past year, 900,000 immigrants have flocked to our shores through the open gates upon our eastern coast.

They come according to some accounts at the rate of 5,000 a day. They come not full-fledged American citizens, but many of them strangers to our institutions and laws. Many of them are as illiterate and bigoted as, and less industrious and honest than, the Chinese, against whom we have barred our western gates. This constant influx of foreigners must necessarily affect our American civilization. But how does it affect the Church? Can she keep pace with the overwhelming growth of our country population? Here again let reliable statistics speak. But, in order that we may not weary you, with a dry list of figures, allow us to give you a few summarized facts. According to the best available statistics, the number of communicants in our Evangelical Churches in 1800 was 7 per cent. of the population. In 1850, 15 per cent; in 1870, 17 per cent: in 1880, a little over 20 per cent. The increase in population since 1800 has been ninefold, that in Evangelical communicants has been twenty-seven fold —three times as great as the population.

Thus you see, that it is beyond all controversy, that the Church has not only kept abreast of the progress of the age, but in a decade, when the population has been swollen by vast streams of immigration from every part of the world, the advance of the Church has far outstripped the increase of a population, that is unprecedented in the world's history.

But the increase of our material resources is as astonishing, as our increase in population. The wealth of our country has quadrupled in thirty years. "Every sun that rises on American shores," says an English writer, "sees $2,500,000 added to the accumulated capital of the republic, or *one third* of the daily accumulation of mankind.

"Every twenty years," says Senator Hoar. " adds to the proper valuation of this country enough to buy the whole German Empire, with its buildings, ships and invested funds." One-fifth of this property is in the hands of Christians. Why is this? There is a most intimate connection between obedience to divine law and material progress. The people, who walk in the ways of truth and righteousness, shall be exalted among the nations of the earth. England and America would not be to day those mighty factors in the world's history, if it were not for the permeation with this Gospel leaven. It is this, which truly ennobles a people and increases its physical and material comforts, as well as spiritual blessings.

When we look out upon our country to-day, we see the stupendous growth of the mustard-seed most strikingly illustrated before our eyes. What are these earthly millions, who come from the most distant shores, driven by want or oppression, to our highly favored Christian land, but the birds flying to the mustard-tree for food and shelter among its branches? They would not come, if they did not see, that God and his blessing were with us. Why do not immigrants throng heathen shores? Ah, there is no comfort, peace or happiness found in an idolatrous or atheistic land. Who of those living in this community, whose shadow never darkens our Church doors, would want to stay here, if these Churches were removed, these Bibles destroyed, and all religious sentiments excluded from social life? Is it not true, that those, who oppose Christianity most violently, unconsciously seek shelter beneath its delightful shade?

But, in order to measure the growth of the Church, we must go abroad, for its branches, like those of Joseph's bough, run over the wall. The Church is no longer confined to a few lands upon the map of the world, but the banner of the cross has been planted upon the remotest shores. The messengers of the Gospel have entered through the open portals of China and Japan. The dismal jungles of India are radiant with Gospel light and civilization, and the beams of Bethlehem's star are penetrating through the thick gloom of Africa's midnight darkness.

Wonderful changes have taken place upon heathen soil. Where a few years ago cannibalism with all its horrors prevailed, we now find an industrious and peace-loving people. Upon the old slave market of Zanzibar, where not less than thirty thousand slaves were sold annually, we find to day a thriving Church and growing mission school.

Of the 120,000 inhabitants of the Feegee Islands, 102,000 are attendants on public worship. Well may Dr. Barth, one of Germany's greatest champions of missions sing:

> "Where we hardly dared to hope,
> Now the doors stand open wide;
> Slow and faint we only grope,
> Following thy victorious stride."

We have noticed how rapid the growth of the Church is at home, but this has no comparison with its growth among the uncivilized races. It is a very low estimate to say, that it is from four to five times greater, with a ministerial force two-thirds less.

(2)

In some parts of the heathen field there has been an actual return of Pentecost, and it became almost literally true, that a nation was born in a day.

More than seven millions and a half Dollars are annually contributed by the Church for the support of missions. But its returns are ample, and not a cent is wasted. Why, my brethren, it is a fact, which is open to every man's investigation, that it costs more than a seventh less to save a pagan sinner, than it does to save a christian sinner. But missions pay even from a financial and scientific point of view. Would commerce be what it is to-day, and would the cause of science and education not suffer a marked decline, if the Church should cease to lengthen her cords and strengthen her stakes? "Few are aware," says the great Agassiz "how much we owe to missionaries for both their intelligent observation of facts, and their collecting of specimens." Again he says: "We must look to them not a little for aid in our future efforts for the advancement of science." Dr. Moffat says, that when he went as a missionary to South Africa, not a pound's worth of British goods were sold, where hundreds of thousands of pounds worth are now sold.

A missionary in Eastern Turkey is reported as having ordered from America more than a hundred fanning mills for the natives among whom he labored.

The Sandwich Islands were evangelized at a cost of a million and a quarter, and our commerce with them yields every year a clear profit of five millions. This work pays in Dollars and cents. God is so anxious for the means to carry forward this work, says, Dr. Fowler, "that he pays ten per cent. a month to every people, that will advance his cause."

Why all this building of steamships, and railroads? Why all this net-work of telegraph wires, running in every direction to the most distant countries? Has all this no higher significance than to increase the wealth and intelligence of the world? Yes, indeed! These are the great highways, which God casts up for the march of his victorious army. Through all these wide-spread facilities, the nations are brought at our doors and receive from us the light of revelation, and become the willing subjects of our Heavenly King.

It is truly lamentable, that so many, who boastfully speak of the rapid strides of civilization, fail to observe the invisible hand, which guides these earthly powers to the hastening of his universal sway. How many professing Christians there are, who secretly harbor the views advanced by unfair and prejudiced sceptics, and think, that the Church is gradually losing its high prestige. Is it not a burning shame, that in this age of universal missions, when the victories of the Church are so numerous and decisive, hosts of Christians never lend an ear to the shouts of triumph that fill the air?

The latest accounts of the bloody battles, fought between two opposing nations, are daily read with eager interest. But the great conquests of King Immanuel, which fill the heavenly hosts with enrapturing joy, are passed by unnoticed.

About other enterprises, of infinitely less consequence, they are well informed, and reason intelligently; but about the greatest cause on earth, the wonder of the ages, they know nothing.

My brethren, how can your soul glow with enthusiasm for our Redeemer's cause, and how can you do your part in this grand, undying work, if you do not study its wonderful achievements?

The mustard seed, planted by a divine hand, has already become a mighty tree, and its branches re-echo with the warblings of tuneful birds.

But its growth has only begun. Millions upon millions must still be brought to seek refuge beneath its shade. The growth of Christianity in the world would be still more remarkable, if the Church realized the full measure of her obligation.

And we may well ask, if the Church has accomplished so much in her half sleeping condition, what can she not do, if she fully arouses to the greatness of her opportunities and the utmost of her endeavors. Oh, let us not forget, that while the increase proceeds from God, that we are his husbandmen, and must diligently look after the planting and the watering. How inconceivably more could each one of us do, if our hearts were wholly in this work.

Oh, for an enthusiasm like that, which was witnessed years ago in the city of London, when venerable, gray-headed ministers of the English Church and dissenters, fell weeping into each other's arms in the chapel of Lady Huntington, and, clasping hands over all narrow denominational limits, founded the London Missionary Society.

Oh! for a return of that spirit of cheerful sacrifice, which was witnessed at the ordination of the first four banner missionaries in 1829, when the contribution plates were filled not only with money, but with gold chains, watches, rings and jewelry of all kinds.

My friends, would you see your Church shine with the glow of the morning, then remember your Lord's last commission, and go, preach the Gospel to all nations. History shows, that those churches have been the most vigorous and fruitful, which pushed their labors far out into the white harvest fields of heathen lands. That Church, which only studies its own wants, and neglects the countless millions, extinguishes its own light. The waters of eternal life, which proceed out of the throne of God, like all other waters, in order to be pure and beneficent, must keep flowing. The moment the Church pents them up in selfish channels, it turns itself into a dead sea, on whose shores no green thing grows, and in whose briny waters no creature lives.

Up then, my brethren. Work with all your energies for the Kingdom of Christ, both at home and abroad. Give not merely a few Dollars from your abundance, but give so that you will feel it. You can make no better investment beneath the skies. It insures you an eternal reward in the heavens.

Give towards this best of all causes, not merely your gold and silver, but, like Hannah of old, bring your most beloved Samuels to the altar and say, as this noble mother in Israel did, as long as he liveth he shall be lent to the Lord. Then you will not only bless the remote Pagan, but benefit yourself in the invigoration of your faith and love, and in the development of the highest type of Christian life and character.

Through Death To Victory.

———:———

> Verily, verily, I say unto you, except a corn of wheat fall into the ground and die, it abideth alone; but if it die, it bringeth fourth much fruit.   John 12:24.

E find our Lord for the last time in the city of Jerusalem, where thousands of Jews and Proselytes have gathered to celebrate the annual feast of Passover.

More than ever are all eyes centered upon him.

He has recently performed the most striking miracles, and furnished the most convincing proofs of his divine origin. He has been conducted to Jerusalem's gates, like a king to his coronation amid the waving of palm-branches, and the outbursts of joyful Hosannas. A new honor awaits him here. It appears, that among the vast throng of people, that are in attendance upon this Jewish feast, there are some Greeks, who may have been drawn to this city of the Great King by the rumors of the miraculous powers of this marvellous Galilean prophet, or who may have been, like so many others, "proselytes of the gate."

The country, from which these men came, is renowned to this day for its arts, philosophy and learning. It was the birthplace of eloquence and the cradle of human greatness.

These men, therefore, stand before us as the representatives of the philosophical and the intellectual culture of the world.

But they had grown utterly dissatisfied with the outworn creeds of Paganism, and were anxiously looking for something better and nobler. Their eager eyes were therefore turned to Judaism, and they came to sit down at the feet of Moses and the prophets, to learn "what is happiness," "what is virtue," and "what is the highest good"—questions, which had not been satisfactorily answered in the school of Plato and Arestotle.

These worthy representatives of the highest culture of the age have been eye-witnesses of the great honor conferred upon Christ, and their interest in him has been fully aroused. They would like to know more about him. They would like to have a private interview with him. They do not venture to come into his presence without an introduction. But who shall make them acquainted with this celebrated teacher? Philip, whose Greek name indicates that he is of foreign extraction, is the suitable man to prepare the way for this foreign delegation into the presence of Jesus.

Still, he does not appear before his Master with this petition, until he has consulted with Andrew, his fellow townsman. Who can surmise the feelings, which must have sprung up in the heart of these ambitious disciples?

Another honor for their Master. Shall the Gentile world unite with his own nation in this hour to place the crown of royalty upon his brow?

Whether the Savior held the desired interview with these Greeks, we are not told.

It is rather remarkable, that, at the close of our Lord's earthly career, pagans should come from the West, as at his birth wise men came from the East. The former found his manger, while the latter saw his cross.

The answer, which Jesus gave to this request of the Greeks, is somewhat striking and unlooked for: "The hour is come that the Son of man should be glorified." But not as these earthly minded disciples imagined. Not merely these Greeks, but Pagans from all quarters under the heavens would come to honor the Christ.

But before this can come to pass, he must die a most humiliating death. " Verily, verily, I say unto you, except a corn of wheat fall into the ground and die, it abideth alone; but if it die, it bringeth forth much fruit."

How little these disciples understood this. They looked for earthly glory and worldly pomp.

In all that had transpired during these last few days, and especally in this incident with the Greeks, they found fresh food for their earthly-minded expectations.

Yes, that is the way in which they would have it go.

Yesterday, a joyful Hosanna on the lips of the Jews; a moment ago, a song of praise from the lips of the children; to-day a solemn homage from the Greeks; who knows but what to-morrow they will look upon his throne.

The Savior desires to arouse them out of this sweet dream, lest to-morrow their hearts are broken with the most painful disappointment. Therefore he pictures to them in living colors, his impending death in all it's gloom and horror, as if he meant to say: "Yes, my disciples, your expectation is not unfounded. My coronation is nigh. The hour is come, that the Son of man shall be glorified. But not as ye suppose through the majestic Hosannas of the Jews. or the modest homage of the Greeks, but through my sufferings and death.

A few more sounds of the clock and the streets of Jerusalem will witness an entirely different scene. "Crucify him, crucify him," will be the cry, that shall fall from those lips, which, but yesterday, shouted "Hosanna, blessed is he, that cometh in the name of the Lord," and Jew and Gentile shall join hands in inflicting upon me the most torturing death.

And yet, when your eyes shall look upon these harrowing scenes, remember the words, which I spoke unto you, and say to one another: "Behold the hour has come, that the Son of man is glorified." This deep humiliation is the very pathway to my infinite exaltation, for, " Except a corn of wheat fall into the ground and die, it abideth alone; but if it die, it bringeth forth much fruit."

The Savior lays down this great principle or the universal law, that we attain to a higher and more fruitful life, through dissolution or distruction. The grain must die beneath the warm and moistened clod, before it can assume a nobler form.

The seed would be worthless and could never supply the needs of the hungry millions, unless it were cast in the open furrows and there lose its original form.

1st. This Law Applies First of All To The Life Of Our Savior.

In him it has been strikingly verified. Through dissolution to the highest fruitfulness.

What would have become of Christianity, if these short-sighted disciples had had their own way? They would have sought earthly honor and glory for their Master. They would have loved to have seen him break away from the narrow confines of his labors, until his power and glory should have crowned every hill top on earth.

His work seemed but just begun, and does he now speak of death? For a little more than three years his comforting and cheering words have fallen upon the ears of the distressed and mourning, and his sympathetic hand has touched with healing power the sick and dying; and must he now be stricken down in the midst of his usefulness, with such a bright career before him? "How hard," says Dr. Bacon, "it was for the disciples to see the purpose of this waste." How hard it is for some to-day. So great a teacher and example as he was! These two or three years of public life; these few pages of recorded sayings, how they have blessed the sinful world! How rich the world would have been, if that fair and lovely young life could have been lengthened out, illuminating all the vicissitudes of human joy and sorrow with its blessed light, till it had filled the round of three score years and ten—if the recorded sayings of these holy lips could have been increased to volumes—if the hand, which wrote no syllable but those unknown words upon the ground, soon to be effaced by trampling feet, could itself have given us Gospels and Epistles out of the fulness of his own heart.

Oh the calamity to the world, that shall cut off this divine life from among men!"

Such were men's thoughts; but God's thoughts are infinitely higher.

Our Lord turned away from these Greeks, who came to honor him and surrendered himself to the treacherous Judas, the jealous Caiaphas, and the vacillating, truckling Pilate, saying: "it is not my teaching, that the world needs, but my death; and when I am lifted up on the accursed cross, that will be the grand magnet which will draw, not merely the Greeks, but men of every nationality and kindred to me."

Christ had on one occasion called himself "the bread of life." But in order to be this for a needy world, it was necessary, that he should, like a corn of wheat, fall into the ground and die.

As the farmer cannot expect a waving field of grain, except at the expense of some seed, no more could the Christ expect a harvest of redeemed souls, except at the sacrifice of his own life. From the very opening of his career, therefore, he turned his back to all earthly greatness and that, which the world terms success, and nerved himself for scorn, laceration and buffetings.

Without these he might, after a long and prosperous life, have passed away into glory, and have been immortalized on earth as a marvellous hero and philanthropist; but he never could have reaped the joys, and fruits of a Savior, or Redeemer. Like the unburied seed, he would have remained alone. No single fallen sinner could have rejoiced in his redemption. No mortal child could have passed with him into the joy of heaven. No prodigal could have found such reception beneath the old parental roof.

To redeem us from sin, and to secure rest for the weary, Christ had to close his ears against the Hosannas of earth, and welcome the agonies and shame of the cross. To lead many sons to glory, he had to pass through the dark Kedron Vale; and to draw all to himself with the cords of his matchless love, he must first be nailed to the accursed tree. No disciple, be he Jew or Gentile, could have participated in his glory, save at this tremendous price.

For him, as well as for us, it was true, "no cross, no crown."

It is true, without this humiliating death, he will remain the only-begotten of the Father, full of grace and truth, the person in whom the fulness of the Godhead dwells bodily, the object of angelic delight; but no single sinner will find boldness to approach him, and to none can he be "the bread of life."

But, on the other hand, when he falls like a corn of wheat into the ground and dies, he brings forth much fruit, and we see the words of the prophet strikingly fulfilled "when thou shalt make his soul an offering for sin, he shall see his seed, he shall prolong his days, and the pleasure of the Lord shall prosper in his hand. He shall see of the travail of his soul, and be satisfied."

Who can estimate the fruit, that the death of Christ has borne, and is still bearing? He had scarcely passed from death's dark tunnel, through the portals of the eternal city, when thousands rejoiced in him as their risen Savior.

How many precious sheaves have already been stored away in heaven's safe garner.

How many still stand waiting on the world's outstretched fields to be carried away in their turn. Yes, my friends, lift up your eyes, and are not the fields everywhere white unto the harvest, and do they not loudly call for the sickle?

Whence all these golden fields? Whence all this fruit?

The answer is simply this: The corn of wheat fell into the ground and died and brought forth much fruit. The hour came in which the Son of man was glorified.

And to-day we see not merely civilized Greeks, but the most rude and barbaric nations draw nigh, anxiously saying: "We would see Jesus." Yes, in the distance, we hear the tread of millions, not merely from the Orient and Occident, but from every region and clime under the broad heavens, coming to present their treasures of gold, frankincense and myrrh unto the blessed Christ.

Well may we exclaim in view of the increasing harvest of souls—"Thanks be to the Christ of history, who was willing to suffer temporal defeat, in order that he might be crowned with undying splendor."

2nd. But this principle of the text applies *not to our Lord alone, but to every one, who would be his disciple.*

We are to fall into the ground like a corn of wheat, or, in other words, we are called to pass through dissolution to fruitfulness, through death to life. It is not enough, that we speak admiringly of the Christ. It is not enough, that we are not offended at his death, but we are to be willing to accept his condition as our own, and to pursue the path he trod. We are to be willing to suffer what looks like defeat and shame in the eyes of the world, in order that we may attain to the unfading honors of the skies. Hence the Savior uttered these words, which immediately follow our text: "He that loveth his life shall lose it, and he that hateth his life in this world, shall keep it unto life eternal. If any man serve me, let him follow me; and where I am there shall also my servant be; if any man serve me, him will my Father honor."

We have in these words the same thoughts expressed under altogether different imagery. We are to lose our life, not necessarily our physical life, but our sensual and sinful life, in order that we may attain to that higher life.

We are to die to self, to self-indulgence, self-glory, and self aggrandizement. That selfishness, which comes out so prominently in every human life, must be nailed with Christ to the cross, and we must be able to say with Paul, "*I live* yet not *I*, but *Christ* liveth in me." It has been well said, "If ye will bear fruit, ye too, must make the like surrender—must die to your personal plans, hopes, ambitions; die to your selfish loves and hates; die.—O, last struggle of the best and worthiest souls—die to your longings and purposes of useful service in God's kingdom. so far as these are *your* purposes and not *God's*—that so God may glorify his name in you—yea, and glorify it again."

To the world this looks like a barren and unprofitable life. But it is the royal road to the widest usefulness.

All those, who have attained to true spiritual greatness in the kingdom of God, have pressed the footsteps of their Master in this path of self-abnegation.

O, would that we might never forget what every waving field so loudly declares, that we are not destined to dazzle as a pearl in the crown of a vain world, but to fall like seed to die, and thus become a blessing to others.

What a blessed thought to realize, that we are not living, nor laboring in vain. For a time we may seem forgotten, but our fruit-bearing season draws nigh, and our joy will be boundless.

"The penalty of self-seeking and self-indulgence is, that every selfish man abideth alone." The history of the Christion Church of all ages has been that of the fallen grain, which through dissolution attains to the highest fruitfulness. Hence, the blood of martyrs has been called the seed of the Church.

It was a sad hour in the history of the N. T. Church, when that most excellent deacon Stephen, so full of faith and of the Holy Spirit, fell beneath the pelting stones. It seemed that his untimely death was an irreparable loss to the Church.

But lo! what happens?

Through the persecution, which was now set on foot, the disciples at Jerusalem were scattered in all directions, which, like flaming brands, in a short time set the whole Roman Kingdom ablaze.

Near the spot, where this holy martyr fell, stood a young man, who kept the clothes of the executioners, and witnessed the patience and forgiving spirit of this dying saint, and went home pricked in his heart, destined to carry on, on an infinitely wider scale, the work, which Stephen had been compelled to lay down.

Oh, how often, as we review this history of the past, does defeat and disappointment seem to be the lot of Christ's servants. But their temporary obscurity or humiliation leads them on to a still grander and more permanent success.

From a human point of view the work of that noble missionary, David Brainerd, seemed a complete failure.

That eminent young man, who might have dazzled in other circles, before whom many avenues of usefulness opened up, consecrated himself to the work of missions among the Indians.

As a result of overwork, and want of physical care and comfort, his wasted form was laid in an early tomb. A few score of Swarthy Indian converts was all the fruit of so much toil, prayers and tears. But wait, and the dying seed shall appear, and multiply its fruitfulness. The memorials of this eminently pious missionary were gathered by Jonathan Edwards, who had hoped to call him son, into a book. The little book took wings and fled beyond the sea, and alighted on the table of a Cambridge student, Henry Martyn. Its contents deeply stirred his heart, and he resolved, that he would become a missionary.

He turned his back to fame and worldly greatness, and consecrated his genius and scholarship to God's cause in the heart of heathen degradation.

But how little apparently he had accomplished, when his health broke down, and he was obliged to leave India.

Unable to reach home, he died upon the lonely sea-shore, crouched under piled-up saddles, to cool his burning face by contact with the earth. No Christian friend was at his side to administer relief or to whisper in his dying ear the unfailing promises of his God.

But Henry Martyn's early death was not all loss.

His thoroughly consecrated life aroused the enthusiasm for missions in other hearts—and, as has been well said, "out of that early grave of Brainerd, and that lonely grave of Martyn, far away by the plashing of the Euxine sea, has sprung the noble army of modern missionaries.

The heart of the Christian world has recently been saddened by the martyrdom of Bishop Hannington in Central Africa. What a loss we say is the sudden death of this heroic, Christ-like man! But see, how the death of this fallen grain is bearing ample fruit. Scarcely had tidings of his awful death reached England, when not less than fifty-three of her bravest sons offered themselves to the Church Missionary Society at London, to take the place made vacant by this fallen hero. His very death has become a blessing to the established Church of England, in that it has aroused other hearts, and has given a fresh impulse to the cause of Foreign Missions. The deplored martyrdom of this eminent man has multiplied his influence and power in the Church, and will accomplish for Christ and his Kingdom, what the preservation of his life could never have brought about.

3rd. But the principle of the text is in the last place applicable to *the Christian's physical death.*

It is true, this thought is not expressed in the context.

But who can read these words, without recalling that magnificent chapter in Paul's first letter to the Corinthians, which has been a source of unspeakable comfort to bereaved friends, as they heard the death-clods fall upon the lowered casket, which contained the last remains of a precious friend.

How this beautiful analogy puts to shame the vain arrogance of the haughty caviller.

"But some man will say, how are the dead raised up? and with what body do they come?" "Thou fool, that which thou sowest is not quickened, except it die. And that which thou sowest—thou sowest not that body, that shall be, but bare grain, it may chance of wheat, or some other grain: but God giveth it a body as it hath pleased him, and to every seed his own body."

Deeply humiliating is the thought, that man, who is made but a little lower than the angels, and whom God crowned with honor and glory, and placed over the works of his hands, should within a few years or weeks return to the lap of mother earth.

What a trial it is to commit a faithful father, a tender mother, a much loved companion, the joy of our eyes, or a child, in whom we discern our own image, to the cold and lonely tomb. How painful this knowledge, we shall no more see their faces. We shall never more hear their voices. We shall no longer be able to express our love for them.

How shuddering the thought, that their peaceful remains are every day becoming more dishonored, and gradually become more and more a prey of dissolution.

Alas, how fearfully dark the grave would be, if no bright ray of light fell from heaven upon it.

Our dead, who sleep in Jesus, lie in yonder cemeteries as the seed in the lap of earth, not in order to remain there forever, but in order to awake in God's time to a new and glorious life.

Centuries may roll over our sleeping dust, and it may seem as if this rest would never be interrupted. This once strong and elastic frame may entirely consume to dust, it will never lose its identity or become annihilated. As the grain of wheat cannot pass into a crown of seed, except it fall into the ground and die, so we cannot attain to our glorious resurrection body, without the humiliation of the tomb.

Our dead are therefore not lost, but only sleep, "till the trump of the arch-angel shall arouse them to a higher, glorified life."

Their dust may be precious to us, and may be laid away beneath a profusion of flowers, it cannot be more so, than it is to the Lord Jesus, who bought it with his own precious blood.

Around each grave, he stations a more powerful guard, than the Roman soldiers, who encircled the new tomb of Joseph of Arimathea. Ministering angels, who often carried them invisibly on their hands during their earthly pilgrimage, now hold a faithful watch over their slumbering dust. No field on earth is more promising, than the peaceful resting place of God's holy dead. What a sublime scene that will be, when by-and-bye the sound of the trumpet shall be heard, and the Spirit of the Lord shall come from the four winds of the heavens, and these dead shall live.

Then this body will be forever a stranger to weakness, pain or suffering. Its powers of endurance will no longer be limited, and its range of movement no longer be confined within narrow borders, but it will be made like unto the glorified body of our risen Lord. What a surprising change that will be!

There will be a noticeable resemblance, but not less a striking difference between our present and future body. It was sown in corruption, it shall be raised in incorruption; it was sown in dishonor, it shall be raised in glory; it was sown in weakness, it shall be raised in power.

One body shall resemble the glory of the sun; another the glory of the moon, and another the glory of the stars; and as there is a difference in glory between one star and another, so shall it be in the resurrection of the dead. The redeemed of the Lord shall return and come with singing unto Zion; and everlasting joy shall be upon their head; they shall obtain gladness and joy, and sorrow and mourning shall flee away.

Let the king of terror lay us low; let the worms destroy this body; let the winds blow away the dust of our frail, consuming tabernacle to the four corners of the heavens. God himself will watch over it, and in his own good time renew it according to the working of his power, wherewith he is able to subdue all things unto himself.

And when the Lord Jesus Christ shall appear in glory, and we with him, then we will see this truth fully illustrated, of which we have lisped this morning: "Verily, verily I say unto you, except a corn of wheat fall into the ground and die, it abideth alone; but if it die, it bringeth forth much fruit."

Believer's Treasures.

> Therefore let no man glory in men, for all things are yours; whether Paul or Apollos, or Cephas, or the world, or life, or death, or things present or things to come: all are yours; and ye are Christ's and Christ is God's.
>
> 1 Cor. 3:21-23.

THE Christian Church has never been without its dark blot. Wherever the good seed was scattered, the enemy followed in the darkness of night to sow the injurious tares.

The noblest men and the grandest Church organizations of past centuries come to us tainted with sin and stained with human imperfection. Not even the excellent Church of Corinth formed an exception to this rule.

Its piety was sadly marred by human weaknesses. Sectarianism broke out among them with considerable force, splitting them into different parties or cliques, which called themselves after one of the prominent men, who had labored among them.

This great evil threatened to destroy the usefulness and spiritual power of the Church.

The apostle Paul, with his keen eye, saw the dangers, which threatened God's work in this mighty stronghold of Paganism, and therefore in this first Epistle addressed to the Corinthians he severely condemns this un-Christlike spirit. He exposes its narrowness, and tries to elevate them to a higher and broader plane of Christian observation.

Why should they follow the teachings of one man and praise him to the skies, and look with disdain on those, who were less talented or qualified according to their estimation of men. This was a wrong spirit, in direct conflict with that of the Gospel. Besides, it betrayed their spiritual ignorance and worldly ambition. Paul, therefore, explains unto them the relation in which these several servants of God stand to each other.

They are all cultivating one field, of which God is the owner and husbandman. They are all building at one glorious temple, which is destined to outlive the ages. Why should one workman, even if his part in the great structure is a little more conspicuous, be exalted above the others, without whose toil its massive walls would never rise.

Therefore he penned this important exhortation: "let no man glory in men; for all things are yours; whether Paul or Apollos, or Cephas, or the world, or life, or death, or things present or things to come; all are yours; and ye are Christ's, and Christ is God's."

In this soul-stirring passage, we have *the boundless possessions* of the believer brought to our notice. A thoughful study of it cannot but be profitable. Who can carefully ponder these weighty words, without feeling his spiritual life quickened, and his soul thrilled with heavenly rapture.

The Christian may well be called "the child of a King." He is heir to an inheritance, which is beyond all description. When king Herod promised the charming Salome, that he would give her whatsoever she asked,—even to the half of his kingdom, that seemed a marvellous gift. But what is it, compared with the incalculable riches, which the apostle spreads out before our view. As if he were the treasurer of the Sovereign Ruler of the Universe, and had the key to all his treasure houses, he lays at our feet all the magnificence of heaven and earth as our divinely allotted gift. It is not so much of future things the apostle here speaks. He does not say all things *shall be* yours by-and-bye in the grand consummation of all things, but he uses the present tense—" all things ARE yours." The Christian is even now an actual possessor of all things. Alas, that his faith is often so weak, that he cannot grasp this all-stimulating truth and walk worthily of such high honor.

But he, and he alone, can spread out his hands to the vaulted skies with its countless burning lamps. And then, as he stands upon some lofty summit, he can let his eyes roam over the hills and valleys, the teeming cities with all their stored gold, and magnificence of art, and say "these are all mine."

That the apostle understood how much it meant, when he said: "all things are yours"—is evident from the different parts of the Christian's wealth which he specifies.

First of all in the list of their royal possessions stand the illustrious men, who have labored among them in word and doctrine —"All things are yours whether Paul or Apollos or Cephas."

"They had said "I am of Paul, and I of Apollos, and I of Cephas." But he turns it right around and says "you are not of them, but they belong to you"—not simply *some one* of them, but *every one* of them. Yours is Paul with his resistless logic and broad catholic spirit; Appollos with his chaste and refined eloquence; Cephas with his matchless heroism—all laboring together for your spiritual edification. Yours are the planters and founders of the christian faith, like Paul and Peter—or the waterers, and gatherers, like Apollos, Timothy, and scores of others.

Yours are those, who have personally labored among you, like Paul and Apollos, or whose faces you have never seen, but of whose burning words and devotion to the Master you have learned from others.

Yours are all their natural endowments and spiritual gifts. Yours their splendid achievements and glorious career—not as a cause of exultation in them, but as a means of thanksgiving to God.

Do not idolize them. Do not wrangle over them. But use them for the purpose for which God gave them.

Great as was this part of the riches of the early Christian Church, ours is ten-fold more so.

To us belongs that long line of celebrated prophets and apostles.

Ours are the martyrs, whose sacred blood has flowed in copious streams to prove the power of the Gospel, even to do and to dare. Ours are the reformers who by their heroism and loyalty to truth have done the Church incalculable service. Ours are all the treasures of the Church fathers of different centuries, whose ample stores of knowledge and christian experience are an inexhaustible mine of wealth to the Church of the future. Ours are the servants of God, no matter in what period of the world, or in what portion of Christ's Kingdom they toil.

Why should any one among us boast—"I am of Luther, I of Calvin and I of Wesley." These men belong not to one particular sect or denomination, but to the whole Church. How great is this part of our spiritual heritage!

As we grow bewildered, when we attempt to number the stars that twinkle in the firmament in a bright clear winter night, so we utterly fail to enumerate all those glittering luminaries, that have gemmed the horizon of the Christian Church. The longer we gaze the more of them come to view. There are Paul and Peter, and John and Timothy, and Polycarp and Chrysostom, and Augustine and Athanasius, and Luther and Latimer, and Calvin and Knox, and Wesley, and Whitefield, and McCheyne and Burns, and Edwards and Payson, and Nettleton and Harlan Page. But where should we end, if we should enumerate them all? Besides, it is not to these alone, that we are greatly indebted. Eternity will reveal what blessed and far-reaching influences for good were set on foot by those, who toiled in utter obscurity.

As the coral builders work beneath the waves for ages, and there lay the foundation of flowing islands, so many are doing splendid work for Christ of which the world never hears.

The saints of the past and the present, therefore, with all their achievements, constitute a part of our glorious possession. Let us make the most of their trials and conquests, of their sowing and reaping, of their influence and example—realizing that they have been given us for our moral and spiritual improvement.

2. *The world* is the next item of the Christian's glorious estate,

as seen by Paul's spiritual vision. You remember how the tempter came to our Lord, in the desert, and spread the glories of the whole world before him, and said; "all these will I give thee, if thou wilt fall down and worship me." But the Lord refused this offer, in order that by his obedience, suffering and death, he might secure it for us. If he had listened to the tempter's voice, we would never have come into possession of it, but now it is ours by Christ's conquest and indisputable right.

"Yours is the world!" Ah, this seemed a singular assertion in Paul's day—and especially from his lips—a man, who owned not a solitary foot of ground, who by stern toil in the sweat of his brow earned a scanty meal.

What hold had the Church made upon the world. What an insignificantly small fragment of its population had embraced its doctrines! Was not the Church persecuted, scourged and thrust out by the world, and yet the apostle in the triumphant tones of faith declares she is ours.

And even to-day, with all the conquests of Christianity, with its rapid growth at home and abroad, it hardly seems according to truth to say "the world is ours."

Does it not seem to be governed by the powers of darkness, and while truth and righteousness here and there attain a victory, is this not set off by still greater triumphs of our spiritual adversaries?

It is true, the world sometimes presents a gloomy aspect, even to the most hopeful optimist, but we should never forget, that our Master has said: "I have overcome the world."

It is his, and therefore ours. We may not be able to grasp why he should allow wickedness to assume such huge proportion, and to make such gigantic strides. We shall understand by-and-bye. We see the wrong side now of the fabric, that will presently come from heaven's loom.

Let us rest assured, that the world is ours. That everything is working together for the good of God's people and the establishment of his kingdom. It has been well said: "The world is ours, a deed of it is lodged in the chancery of Heaven, for we are heirs, joint-heirs with Christ."

The world is ours, Christ bought it for us, and he sanctifies us by his Spirit, so that we learn to use, and not to abuse it. The wicked may be here on every hand. It is not theirs, they are merely permitted to dwell here. For a while he may be in great power and spread himself like a green bay-tree, yet he will speedily pass away and lo, he will not be found. But the meek shall inherit the earth, and they shall eternally possess it. The world is ours! What an inspiring thought this is! .

Ours is its history, ours are its vast resources. Its fertile fields, its well-stored mines. Ours are the triumphs of art, the achievements of science, the products of mind, yea, whatever is valuable in this wide world. It bears the stamp of the believer's possession. For him this world revolves upon its axis.

For him this great progress, and these marvellous developments—of these later centuries. All are his Father's gift to him. Why should he therefore lose himself in acquiring a few treasures, while all have been given him.

3. The next possession of the child of God, as mentioned by Paul, is *life*.

Yours is *life*. The one thing, that strikes us as we look around us in this universe, is its ceaseless activity.

All is life and stir. This mysterious gift of life also belongs to Christ's blood-bought people. Once they were dead, now they have been quickened by the Holy Spirit, and are alive unto God. Once their life seemed dull and aimless; now it is full of significance and spiritual joy. They turn the golden hours of their present existence to the very best of purposes. They make the most of their entrusted talents and their thousand-fold opportunities.

Their spiritual life is constantly increasing. They go from strength to strength. But they do not simply possess that little fragment of life, which has been kindled in their own souls; all life is theirs. To quote the words of another: " The complete fulness of the spiritual life, which appeared in Christ; all the workings of the Holy Spirit in countless hearts; every enlightening, every conversion, every progress in holiness, wherever attained, if even in the farthest corner of the earth; for all work together to the perfecting of the kingdom, which is reserved for you."

4. But not only life, in all its force, is a part of the Christian's inheritance, but even *death*, its counterpart, is his. How strange it seems, that the apostle places this among the treasures to which we have fallen heir. Can it be considered as such? Does it not come as a disturber of our peace? Does it not spread gloom and sorrow all around us?

And yet, my friends, the Christian places death on his list of blessings. He does not associate it with the pall, the shroud, and the dark tomb. It is not an interruption of his joy, a defeat of his plans and calculations, but a realization of his hopes and prospects. As death approaches, he does not say "hast thou found me, O mine enemy," but he welcomes him as a white-robed angel, who looses his chains and sets his soul forever at liberty. Death is a terrible word to him, who has no hope in Christ. But to the believer, its sting has been removed, and he regards it as the fiery chariot of the prophet, which conveys him to the everlasting paradise.

Death is ours. This is shown by those innumerable happy death-beds, around which the very glory of heaven was reflected. If time permitted, we might tarry by the side of some, as the end had come, and listen to the rapturous strains of song and testimony that fell from their lips. Said one: "This is the brightest and best hour of my life: I'm swimming in glory."

It is only the Christian, who can say "death is mine—I am its conqueror—I dread not its bitterness, for through these dark portals my Savior has passed, and he has left a pathway of glory behind."

4. But the apostle is not through yet with enumerating our possessions. Time would fail him, if he should go into details; therefore he summarizes—*things present* are yours. "Everything, that exists, and *as* it exists, is for your good. You may cry out in anguish of heart—as one after another of your children is snatched from your side—"all these things are against me;" or you may say as you go, stooped with heavy burdens and crushed with

disappointments, "call me Marah, for the Almighty hath dealt bitterly with me."

Yes, the repetition and the violence of God's chastisements may so completely overcome you, that you fairly question the justice of God. Yet, notwithstanding all these things— *all things* are yours.

These very reverses are but blessings in disguise. It is your ignorance alone, that evokes complaint; if you could see the bearing of these present providential visitations upon your future life, your heart would praise God for them. Whatever, therefore, God sends to us, whether it be joy or sorrow, prosperity or adversity, triumph or defeat, thorns in the flesh or exhaltations into the third heaven—let us never forget the confident, Pauline assertion: "all things are yours."

And now, after the apostle has called our attention to all things present as they exist in the individual life, in the family, Church, State and the world, and has pronounced them as being ours, working out, in spite of apparent contradiction, our highest good, he brings his survey of the believer's possessions to a close by calling his attention to future things.

Present afflictions or crosses may often distress us—but the sharpest pain, perhaps, is anticipated evil. How often we run ahead and add, to the burdens of to-day, those of to-morrow.

How many a one is greatly disturbed in his mind, not on account of something that has happened, but that possibly may happen. The future of the child of God is all radiant and bright —" for all things to come are his."—What the apostle wrote to the Philippians with regard to his bonds, we may say with reference to everything that may befall us; "for I know that this shall turn to my salvation." Everything that shall happen to you in the future will only enhance your happiness and increase your glory. We may well, therefore, leave the future entirely in God's keeping—knowing that it will bring nothing, that is not supremely good for us. Why therefore shall we go through life with despondent hearts, knowing what God has purposed concerning us. Put away, therefore, all clouds from your brow, and all anxieties out of your heart, and walk with confident steps, knowing that the future will be brighter than the past, and that the Lord has preserved the best wine of the feast until the last.

"Thine are not only all the former and present things," says Dr. Christlieb, "but also all the future; thine the new heaven and the new earth, thine all the promises and their glorious fulfilment; thine all the battles, and therefore, also the coming, final one between light and darkness, and the mighty victory of light, eternal peace, the unending rest of the people of God!

Thine are the angels and all the blessed in the New Jerusalem; thine all the glory of God and Christ in the world of light; for thee shine all the stars in this life and the next, for thee are rising the enduring mansions of the heavenly home."

When we take even a brief and rapid survey of the Christian's possessions, with what joy our hearts ought to thrill. Why are we not more joyful? May this not be due to the fact, that we are too much shut up in ourselves, and have not unreservedly yielded up ourselves unto Christ. For, remember, there is a limit to the Christian's inheritance—a condition with which we must comply, if we wish to inherit all things.

2. Listen, therefore, to the *exception*, which is made to his boundless estate. There is only one solitary exclusion. "All things are yours, but ye are Christ's and Christ is God's. Yourself is the exception which the apostle makes. You are not your own. You are Christ's property. It is only in and through him, that you can have this fulness of wealth of which we have spoken. But you can never have it on any other condition, than a total surrender of yourself to the Lord Jesus Christ.

And right here is where many come short. They would like all these different parts of the believer's possessions, but not at such a price. They cling to self—and it seems a tremendous sacrifice to them—to put themselves wholly in Christ's hand, to have no will but his, and to make his glory the supreme object of life. And yet, where this surrender is made, what glorious compensation follows. The Christian life is the most blessed servitude! for when we have truly given ourselves to Christ, we are free indeed.

We cannot be our own masters; a surrender must be made, if we desire to taste the sweetness and blessedness of the Christian life. Christ did not belong to himself. He was sub-ordinate to his Father. "Lo, I have come to do the will of God," was the spirit, which he manifested from first to last. His submission was perfect. He was obedient unto death, even the death of the cross. A similar self-surrender is required on our part. We must become Christ's, if we shall become joint-heirs with him to this glorious estate. We must give him our heart, our intellect, our will, our time, our money or talents. Nothing may be withheld from him. We should say in the spirit of Miss Frances R. Havergal:

"Take my life and let it be
Consecrated Lord to thee;
Take my hands and let them move,
At the impulse of thy love.

Take my feet and let them be
Swift and beautiful to thee;
Take my voice and let me sing
Always—only—for my King.

Take my lips and let them be
Filled with messages for thee;
Take my silver and my gold,
Not a mite would I withhold.

Take my moments and my days
Let them flow in endless praise;
Take my intellect and use
Every power as Thou shalt choose.

Take my will and make it Thine,
It shall be no longer mine;
Take my heart, it is Thine own,
It shall be thy royal throne.

Take my love, my God, I pour
At Thy feet tts treasure store;
Take myself and I will be
Ever, only, all for Thee."

Such consecration of ourselves does Christ deserve. Has he not the most sacred claim upon all our lives. Has he not made—has he not kept us to the present hour, and loaded us with his benefits? Has he not redeemed us at a tremendous cost? What shame then to withhold ourselves from him.

Let the thought of his gracious condescension, that he is ready and willing to receive us in all our pollution and sin, melt our hearts into infinite tenderness. Let every idol be cast from the throne of our hearts. Let every abomination be scourged from the shrine of our soul, and let it ever be only filled with his incense. Let us make the sacrifice of ourselves complete; and as God has withheld nothing from us, but has given us all things, let him have the little all that we have to give. Do you refuse to do this? Then remember that you forfeit all this paternal estate—for it is promised only on this condition, that you yield yourselves to Christ. If you do not belong to him, you have nothing, nothing at all; nay, more, you are then exposed to the most fearful condemnation. You may smile at us, and call yourself rich. You may have great worldly possessions, broad acres of land, large possessions. You may call your lands after your own names, and boast in the multitude of your riches. Your inward thought may be, that your houses shall continue forever, and your dwelling-places to all generations. But you are simply a steward, not an owner.

These possessions are only entrusted to you for a time, and if you prove unfaithful—if you only use them for your own comfort, and administer them for yourself, and not for the honor of your Master, and in the proper channels he has marked out, you shall be punished as a wicked steward—guilty of wasting his Lord's goods. Every minute that you divert from the true purpose of life, every heart-throb that is withheld from him, increases your guilt. Look at your condition as described in these veritable pages. You are a miserable pauper with all your wealth—if you are not truly Christ's. The future is not yours. O, how you dread the future world. The present is not yours, for it is fast melting away under your hands, and is ripening you for a harvest of eternal woe. Death is not yours, for you tremble as you think. that this fell destroyer is silently but surely approaching, and that soon he will lead you out to his narrow home. Life is not yours, for you do not know what true life is, and hence questions like these will arise in your mind: "is life worth living?" The world is not yours, for you do not use it for the purpose that God intended; and the divinely commissioned teachers, who un-unfold unto us the oracles of God, are not yours, for you do not give heed to their instructions, but perish in sinful disobedience and transgression of God's commandments. The blessings of grace and time, which are measured out to you by the second, are rapidly slipping away from you.

Soon you will stand before your Maker, completely stripped of everything. Will you go on in this perilous course? This day look into your spiritual condition and heed the voice of God, which is so tenderly calling you.

Give yourself unreservedly to Christ, in order that you may become an heir of eternal life, a participant of that glory, which never fades away.

The Sabbath.

> If the foundations be destroyed, what can the righteous do.   Ps. 11:3.

WE live in perilous times. The rapid growth of the population of this country; the socialistic and communistic elements, that come to these shores from the old world, jeopardise some of the noblest and approved institutions of this land.

For several years back there has been a lamentable decline in the strictness of our Sabbath observances.

Our Sabbath laws have been disregarded and trampled upon with impunity.

Gradually the hallowed stillness of the Sabbath has been broken, and our streets and thorough-fares are crowded on that day with excursionists, and pleasure-seekers.

Our cities on that day assume the aspect of a national holiday, rather than that of one devoted to the worship of God, and the moral improvement of the people.

O, how these grand old puritan fathers, who laid the broad and deep foundations of this glorious Republic, would stand amazed and shocked, if they could witness the sad spectacle of our modern Sabbath. But the work of deterioration is not going on rapidly enough in the estimation of some. They would do away with the Sabbath altogether, if not in name, yet in reality. They have organized themselves under the high-sounding name, of "personal liberty party." They desire to have part of our liquor laws repealed, and to have the saloon open on the Lord's day. They demand a pledge from the candidates for the legislature, that they shall vote for such measures, and they have solemnly purposed not to cast their vote for any candidate at our coming election, who shall not positively commit himself to such a course of action. Back of this strongly organized party stands the whole liquor traffic with all its satanic shrewdness and increasing power.

The chances, that they will carry their point and that we shall have open saloons on the Sabbath, not as now saloons open in spite of the law, but under its protection—are greater than many a one imagines.

Who knows not the weakness of our politicians, who only ask which course of procedure will secure them the strongest support at the ballot box.

Many of our noblest citizens, foreseeing this evil, have taken strong measures, if possible, to counteract this movement, which threatens to take possession of our Sabbath. In all our larger cities mass meetings are being held to oppose this "personal liberty" party, and to expose the force, which lies behind this entire movement, and the appalling danger, which threatens us. Ministers of all Protestant and Catholic churches, who regard God's holy Sabbath as a grand bulwark of this Republic, are rising up en masse to denounce and counteract this subtle movement. To-day the various pulpits throughout the land are sounding forth the note of alarm, and are calling every worthy citizen to a consideration of his duty in this critical hour.

While I am the last man, that would indulge in political discussions in the pulpit, yet I am reminded, that this is not so much a question of politics, but solely and purely of morals. The minister, as God's watchman upon the walls of Zion, when he sees dangers approaching, that not merely threaten the life and prosperity of the nation, but also the very existence of God's Church, is unfaithful to his holy charge, if he do not sound the trump of alarm, and arouse the hosts of the living God from their fatal slumbers.

What will be the result for our country, our Church, and our homes, if this personal liberty party see their concerted plans carried out?

Who does not feel to-day like Nehemiah, who sat down and wept, and mourned, and fasted, and prayed before the God of heaven at the sight of the demolished walls, and the consumed gates or Jerusalem—when we observe how God's holy and beneficent ordinances are trodden under foot, and iniquity rules with a high and daring hand.

What a sad sight presents our modern Sabbath, compared with that of years gone by. But what will it be, if the measures of this personal liberty party are enacted, and we have free rum on the Sabbath. Can you imagine anything worse than closed shops and stores and offices, but open saloons, inviting the working men to dissipation and wickedness. Is it not enough, that these breathing-holes of hell deal out their liquid fire and damnation for six days of the week? Must they also have God's holy Sabbath day? Can they not ruin our young men fast enough in six days out of seven—but must they also have that day, when they can spend their unbroken time in the dram-shop—where no bells or whistles call them away from their dissipation? Who can picture the pandemonium into which society will be turned, if we have open saloons on the Sabbath.

What an increase of disorder and lawlessness. What an advance in the worst forms of vice and crime. What a neglect of family interest, and what a decrease of the attendance upon the regular Church services.

Thousands of our working men, who now spend their Sabbath with their families at home, will then hang around the saloons, and those, who now resume the weekly toil on Monday morning with fresh vigor and recruited energies, will then be worse for the Sabbath they have enjoyed.

"A Sunday well spent
Brings a week of content,
And health for the toils of the morrow.
But a Sabbath profaned,
Whatsoe'er may be gained,
Is a certain forerunner of sorrow."

The miseries, both physical and moral, which such an enactment will bring upon the American people, beggars all description.

Standard German authors assert that in their Sabbath-less land the larger proportion of criminal and disgraceful acts is committed on Sunday, such as immorality and drunkenness. Many a maiden has lost her virtue on that day; many a youth has seized the murderous knife. Most of the suicides occur on "blue Monday."

We think even now that the miseries and crimes resulting from strong drink are sufficiently appalling, but we have no conception of what hangs over our heads, if this new party prove victorious in this intense struggle.

May God prevent this, for the woes of intemperance are already more than enough.

But have these foreigners no right to ask or to demand the enactment of such laws on the ground of personal liberty?

This they claim.

But what is personal liberty? Does it mean that a person can do just what he wants to? This seem to be the idea, which some have of individual liberty. But this is altogether a false idea. For the benefit of living in society we are bound to surrender some of our personal liberties. To the ignorant, liberty is an unfenced prairie of license and lawlessness, but to the intelligent, it is bounded on every side, like a circle, by the rights of others.

An entelligent working-man of foreign birth once said, that the conception of liberty, which is generally, though not universally, held in the steerage of the ocean steamers, that ply between European Monarchies and the American Republic, is that one can do whatever he pleases in the land of the free. But they are usually quickly cured of these erroneous conceptions.

About the first thing, that they learn here, is the lesson of obedience, for without this, no free republic can exist. Before the foot of the immigrant presses American soil, he learns that under this free government he is subject to law, as well as under the monarchical sway from which he comes.

Before he is at liberty to land, the health officer of the harbor comes on board to ascertain whether there is a contagious disease on board, and if so, they are quarantined. After having settled they speedily learn, that they cannot do just what they please.

They may put their children to work, but they are soon sent home and they are reminded, that they are not permitted to let them grow up in ignorance, because ignorance endangers the life of the nation.

They may attempt to open a lottery, but they discover very soon, that the American laws forbid this, as gambling is found to be a species of robbery, and is one of the demoralizing influences, that endanger the very existence of society. If these new comers happen to be Turks, and try to keep a polygamous harem, the law is quickly upon their heels, and they are taught, that it is forbidden, because it destroys our pure homes and our national virtue.

The longer these immigrants are in the country, the more they learn in how many different ways their liberty is checked. The law aims at the good of the whole, even if it cost sacrifice on the part of the individual. On this ground also our Sabbath laws are founded. We have these laws, not because the religious part of the community forced them upon the State, but because experience had taught those, who founded this government, that its best interest and its continued prosperity require them. Let no one, therefore, imagine, that the Church has hushed these wheels in the factory on the Sabbath day, and has covered the merchandise on the shelves; the Church lays no oppressive burdens on the working classes, but gently seeks to lead them to God. The Sabbath with its cessation from toil, and with its institutions for mental and moral improvement, is founded on the very needs of society, and he, who tries to undermine or overturn this most beneficent of all institutions, is no liberty-loving patriot, but a traitor and revolutionist.

The great danger, that threatens the overthrow of our American Sabbath, rises from the large number of foreigners, that come flocking to these shores. They do not understand the nature and genius of American institutions.

They are not in sympathy with them. All they want is wealth and pleasure. They use every means within their power to destroy the sanctity of the Sabbath, and to convert it into a day of

(4)

mere pleasure or vicious indulgence. Year by year these foreign elements are increasing, and they are becoming more and more an organized power. Already they have made desperate attacks upon this consecrated day of rest. In many of our* great cities the Sabbath is virtually gone. It has become an uproarious holiday. From morning till night, the theatres and museums are crowded with spectators, while the horse-races and base-ball performances are only measured by the capacity of the accommodations.

These enjoyments on the Sabbath necessitate the labor of thousands--who are driven on this day more than on any other. But these pleasure-loving foreigners are not satisfied with the liberties they have, and they now demand of those, whom they put in office, that they shall do away with these Sabbath restraints, and give them an open dram-shop as on any other day.

This demand is as unjust as it is perilous. We cannot give up our Sabbath, because it is God's day.

It is not an offspring of Christianity. It is as old as the race. It was not called into being by Moses—but by God himself, and it has existed from the days of Paradise. Upon its proper observance the happiness and prosperity of the race have ever depended. It has been rightly remarked: "The Sabbath was linked with the birth of the world, with the birth of revelation, and with the birth of the resurrection. Instead of being abrogated, it was universally and perpetually obligatory.

Nocturnal rest was not enough for man. Physiological laws demanded its observance, and its effect could be observed in cattle and horses as well as in man.

In former times, when there were no railroads to bring cattle to the market, and when it was the custom to bring them in droves on foot, kind herders had discovered, that better time could be made, and that the cattle could be brought in in better condition, when they were given their Sunday rest, than when it was denied them.

The necessity of one day of seven, given to physical rest, stands enstamped on the very constitution of the human race. Those nations have prospered the best, that were faithful and rigid in the keeping of the Sabbath.

But where this pearl of days was treated with seeming neglect, and devoted to labor and amusement, deterioration followed. That was a very significant remark of Emerson's that Sunday is "the core of our civilization." Let us see to it, that we do not lend our influence in poisoning that core by permitting it to degenerate into a high carnival of sport, dissipation and enslaved drudgery.

If time allowed, we might give you the opinions of some of the greatest men, that have adorned the annals of this age and country—how they regarded the observance of this weekly restday. Blackstone has said "Shut up the American Church and abolish the American Sabbath, and you shut up the chiefest fountains of truth; Christianity and true republicanism cannot exist upon a platform of infidelity."

Mark Hopkins has left these words on record: "History confirms the position, that the enemies of freedom and of the Sabbath have been the same. A holiday Sabbath is the ally of despotism."

Voltaire was quite right, when he said he would never destroy christianity, unless he could destroy Sunday. But when this has been once accomplished, its downfall is almost sure.

A great Catholic statesman has made the remark, that, without a Sabbath, we have no worship, and without worship, we have no religion.

And years gone by when our peaceful Sabbath attracted universal attention, a French writer is reported to have said: "France must have the American Sabbath or she is ruined."

We might multiply these testimonies, which express the firm conviction of the brightest intellects of all time, that the Sabbath is the conservator of our liberties, and the great bulwark of Christianity. Obliterate it or let it become an institution of the past, and there is nothing that can save this nation from anarchy or utter ruin. Well may we therefore call upon every freedom-loving patriot to guard with zealous care this most beneficent of all our institutions.

The celebrated statue of Troy was called from Pallas—the palladium; it was regarded as the talisman, on whose preservation hung the safety of the capitol. So confident were the Trojans in the power of its presence that, while it remained in the citadel, the citizens braved a siege of ten years; but when by Diomede and Ulysses the image was stolen, they gave way to despair, feeling that all was lost, as did the Jews, when they saw the marble and the gold of their temple wrapped in a winding sheet of flame.

It has been well said: "If there be any real Palladium to the Christian commonwealth, any gift of God, that has come down from heaven to stand in the midst of the State, as the talisman of our national life, it is the Christian Sabbath. Enshrine that in the popular heart, and all else is comparatively safe.

About the Sabbath cluster all religious interests. It is linked with an open sanctuary and an open Bible; with the worship of God and the works of piety; and while Sabbath-keeping is encouraged, all these grand agencies of religious development and moral culture are a thousand-fold more potent. But rudely or recklessly break down the sacred limits, which enclose the day of God—and holy homes and holy places, and holy things are alike exposed to the trampling feet of the scoffer and the skeptic, the irreligious and the infidel. A blow is struck at national prosperity, national morality—national perpetuity."

But what is true with regard to the nation as a whole, is also true with respect to every individual of it. "A corruption of morals," says Blackstone, "usually follows a profanation of the Sabbath. A man, who committed a murder, was tried, found guilty, and condemned to be hanged. A few days before his execution upon the walls of his prison he drew a gallows, with five steps leading up to it.

On the first step he wrote, *disobedience* to parents. On the second step, *Sabbath breaking*. On the third step, *gambling* and *drunkenness*. On the fourth step, *murder*.

Justice Stong, of the U. S. Supreme Court, has said: "Those, who have observed the administration of criminal law or been familiar with prison discipline, have often heard the sad confession of a convicted criminal, that his career downward commenced with Sabbath desecration."

An aged clergyman in Baltimore states, that during the many years he was Chaplain to the Maryland Penitentiary, he took great pains to find out from the convicts, what was the commencement of their downward course; and the testimony of ninety-nine out of a hundred was, that the beginning of their wicked courses was breaking the Sabbath.

We might multiply these testimonies of reliable witnesses to a considerable extent, but we must forbear.

No one can sit down and calmly think of this subject without coming to the conclusion, that the Sabbath is indeed the poor man's friend, and productive of incalculable temporal and spiritual good.

A gentleman one day walking near a Pennsylvania coal mine saw a field full of mules. The boy, who was with him, said: "There are the mules, that work all the week down in the mine, but Sunday they have to come up into the light, or else in a little while they become blind." In like manner, we, who are toiling hard six days of the week in the mines of worldly cares and earthly pursuits, need at least one day in a week in which we climb to the hill-tops, to have our vision clarified and train ourselves for the glory that lies beyond. Without this weekly preparation, we can rest assured, that we shall never enter the rest that remaineth for the people of God.

We have sufficiently shown by these few hasty remarks, what an invaluable blessing the Sabbath is, and that we cannot destroy its sanctity without great peril to ourselves and our homes. From this also we see, what great enemies they are of our liberties, and of all that we value most, who seek to rob us of this our greates national boon. And the question naturally arises, how can we best protect and defend the precious heritage of a Christian Sabbath?

We remark first of all, *let each individual see, that he duly reverence this day.*

Sunday is not a fetich to be worshipped. It is a benefaction from God to be used for man's highest good. "The Sabbath was made for man." It is one of those kind provisions, which our Creator made for us. Let us heartily enter into the purpose and design of this day, and solely use it for that, which it was given for. There is alas! too much Sabbath-desecration—even among the followers of Christ. Many seem to think, that it will do no harm to indulge in a little pleasure on the Lord's day, provided they attend Church in the morning.

Many do not shrink back from imposing burdens upon others on this day, and engage in profitless diversions and needless labors. We would be startled, if we knew the great number of nominal Christians, who break the Sabbath day apparently without the slightest compunctions of conscience. Again and again, we have been told, that our barber-shops and other places of business, that are open on Sabbath, are largely patronized by Church members.

How many disciples of the holy Jesus, who spent the hours of night in communion with his Father—scarcely read and meditate upon God's word at all, but spend the precious hours of this sacred day in reading Sunday newspapers.

With a mind full of the news of the market and the street, with the records of scandal and crime, is it any wonder, that they sit listless in the house of God, and that the Sabbath is a day of weariness to them? O, for some bold Nehemiah in all our pulpits, who would thunder in their ears: "what evil is this that ye do, and profane the Sabbath day." If the Church of the living God had not been so direlict in this duty, things would never have come to such a pass. What our duty is now, is to return with humble confession to God, who is plenteous in mercy, and will abundantly pardon.

But not only as individuals, but also as families, we should be more strict in the observance of this day.

There has been a growing laxity in this regard. The change, which has come over many a home in the last few decades, is no advance, but is truly sad and startling. Many of us can recall the strictness with which this day was kept in the home of our childhood. How minute and careful was the preparation on Saturday evening, and what real rest and delight the Sabbath brought. It seemed to carry heaven's benediction with it. It filled the home with a fragrance which seemed to waft from Paradise above.

But enter some homes now. All is confusion and unrest. A great share of the forenoon is spent in bed, a part of the time is devoted to some sort of pleasure, riding or visiting, and one hour is spent in the sanctuary, in order to pacify conscience or to keep up a sort of respectability before men. How differently our forefathers observed this day. It was one of spiritual delight—largely devoted to mental and moral improvement. They could most truthfully sing: "Day of all the week the best, emblem of eternal rest."

Let us see to it, that we have good Sabbath regulations in the family. Let us be strict in the enforcement of the fourth commandment, yet not so, that this day shall be dull or burdensome to our children. There are various ways by which we can improve its golden hours, so that they shall be the happiest of all the week. Whatever your children may forget in after life, they will never forget the family altar, where the flame of devotion burned brightly, nor the pleasant Sabbath hours, when the atmosphere of heaven seemed to pervade the home, and God seemed very near.

Lastly, *we should faithfully discharge our duty as American citizens with respect to this day.*

We should firmly stand by our Sabbath-laws, and do what is in our power to see, that they are properly enforced.

We should never surrender.

Young men! I know what are the temptations, that will confront you in this age of loose morals, and indifference to Sabbath observance; and with God's help to-night, I want to fortify you and have you do your best, so that this best of all days is not snatched away from us, but is honored, as God would have it honored.

Let me give you a few examples of those, who were faithful in their Sabbath-keeping, and show you how God's blessing followed them all through life.

Judge Hale, one of England's wisest and best judges, who was also an eminent Christian, said: "Forty years experience and observation about the Sabbath has taught me, that, whenever I undertook any worldly business on the Lord's day, that business never prospered. Nay, I have noticed, that if I ever planned, or thought about any temporal business on that day, it never prospered, so that I was always afraid even to think of any worldly business on the Sabbath."

"Nay, more than this," said he, "I have noticed, that the more diligent and careful I was in attending properly to the duties and privileges of the Lord's day, the more happy and successful I was in my business, during the following week; so that, from the way in which I kept the Sabbath, I could always tell how I might expect to prosper in the employments of the ensuing week."

The testimony of this celebrated man has been put into verse by some one, which reads thus:

"A Sunday well spent
Brings a week of content,
And health for the toils of the morrow.
But a Sabbath profaned,
Whatsoe'er may be gained,
Is a certain forerunner of sorrow."

A faithful minister of the Gospel tells of a young man who came to him, saying "I am in trouble. Please advise me what to do."

"What is the matter, my young friend?" he asked.

His reply was: "My employer wants me to work on the Sabbath, I must either lose my place or break the Sabbath. Now which would you advise me to do?"

Without a moment's hesitation he said. "Why, let your place go, and honor God's holy day. If you think, my friend, that God can't open another door as quickly and as widely, as that which your employer can shut against you, then you might hesitate. But you know he can, and I feel sure he will. Trust him and do what you know is right." The young man took his advice. He gave up his place and honored God by trusting in him. The result was none other than that, which we would naturally expect of God, who has so solemnly declared, that he will honor them, that honor him. More than twenty years have elapsed since that day. But that young man now has the title of Honorable attached to his name. He has been greatly prosperous in business, and is worth more than half a million of Dollars—God's mark of approval on the keeping of his day.

Here is another instance, which proves, that God will bless those who respect his day.

A Christian workman in the employment of a gentleman, who kept a large machine-shop, was addressed thus one Saturday evening, when he received his weekly wages: "John, I want you to be on hand to-morrow morning to push forward the work on that machine, which is to go to South America."

He had been working for his proprietor several years, but never had he made such a request before. He promptly replied: "To-morrow is the Sabbath, Mr. Jones, I cannot work on the Sabbath, without breaking the command of God, and doing violence to my own conscience. " That's nothing to me," said Mr. Jones. " you can stick to your principles as much as you please, but my work must be done. If you can't do it, I shall not need your services any longer."

"Mr. Jones," said he. " have I ever disobeyed you before, and have I not always done my work well?"

"That is nothing to the point," was his abrupt reply, "I ask you to come and work to-morrow. If you do so, it will be all right. If not, I don't want you any more."

The honest workman would rather please God, than his employer, and so lost his situation. This blow came upon him in the dullest season of the year. His wife and children were sick, and all the mills were discharging some of their men.

But he was determined, come what may, to keep God's holy day. Eleven days were spent in seeking work, but all in vain. When he went home in a despondent mood, he offerd this prayer to God: "O, Lord! I have done all I can to get work, but have not succeeded. Thou hast promised, that bread shall be given to thy people and their water shall be sure. Now please open some way for me to get bread and water for myself and family."

Soon after he reached home his old employer called upon him and said: "Have you found any work yet?" He answered "no, but I suppose you don't want me."

"Well, said he, "I think you were pretty stiff in your opinions. But I want you to take up that job, where you left it."

"I will gladly do so," was the reply, "but I cannot work on Sunday—I will gladly work till midnight on Saturdays—but then I must stop." "All right," said he, "you'll never be asked to work on the Sabbath again."

We might multiply these testimonies, which so abundantly prove, that God puts not to shame those, who put their trust in him. Don't you think, that God, who preserved Daniel in the lion's den, and the three heroic young men in the fiery oven—don't you think, that God, who took care of his prophet by the brook Cherith, and afterwards beneath a widow's roof, who heareth the young ravens, when they cry, can take care of you? Make up your mind fully, that you will stand by his commandment and keep his holy day, and let him take the consequences.

An infidel once said to a friend: "I have learned by sad experience, that a curse is sure to follow those, who break the Sabbath."

Young men remember this, and shun all companionship and associations, which may tend to a disregard of this blessed day. Never help surrender, shun all companionship with those, who would surrender this day of days to "the emissaries of Mammon and Bachus and Belial, or to any other devils, who would transform our civilization into a hideous riot of sensuality and drunkenness, and greed and crime," which will be the sure downfall of this glorious Republic. As American citizens, we shall see to it, that we vote for no man, no matter to what political party he may belong, who does not positively declare himself in favor of our Sabbath laws, and who does not pledge himself upon his election to aid in their strict enforcement.

You can better afford to be disloyal to your party, than to your God and to his day, upon which so much for us and our prosperity depends. May the Lord avert the danger, which hovers around us, and may he grant unto us the perpetuation of that day, which has been so rich in temporal and spiritual blessings, and has been the golden ladder along which weary pilgrims mounted heavenward, and entered into communion with the unseen God.

In this hour of conflict, as the powers of sin are marshalling all their forces, may the Spirit of the Lord cast up a banner, and grant us a complete and glorious victory.

The Children of the World and the Children of Light.

———:———

> For the children of this world, are in their generation wiser than the children of light. Luke 16:8 last clause.

OUR text is the moral of one of the most difficult, but at the same time, one of the most forcible parables uttered by our Savior—that of the unjust steward.

Two classes of individuals are here contrasted, "the children of this world," and "the children of light."

The Children Of This World

are those, who mind earthly things, who are not born of the Spirit, and therefore do not look by faith to "an inheritance incorruptible, undefiled, which passeth not away." They are children of the world, inasmuch as they depend upon it for their happiness.

As children resemble their parents so they resemble it. They manifest its spirit. They have adopted its maxims, and carry out its behests. Sad indeed must be the condition of those, who are the children of a world, which lieth in wickedness, and passeth away with the lust thereof.

The Children of Light

are directly opposite. They "were sometime darkness, but now are they light in the Lord." They are children of him, who is the

"Father of lights, with whom is no variableness, neither shadow of turning." They are also called children of the day, in contrast to the children of the world, who are of the night, and of darkness—who "love darkness rather than light, because their deeds are evil." The children of light are those, who have received divine illumination, and now shine as luminaries in the world.

"Children of light." How beautiful the figure! What so pure, so beneficial, so fruitful as light! What an elevating thought, to be in such near relation to him, who is the fountain of light. If the human mind can find no object so low and degrading upon which to fix its affections as the world, it can find none so high and ennobling as God. What a marked distinction, therefore, between the children of the world and the children of light! These two classes are as widely separated as heaven and hell.

It cannot be difficult to see which is superior. It is rather astonishing, therefore, at first to hear our Savior say "the children of this world are wiser in their generation, than the children of light." We must bear in mind, however, that Jesus does not commend *everything* that pertains to them, but he has a *single* quality in view, which he detaches from all their other traits, and holds this up as an example worthy of imitation. We find numerous instances of this kind recorded in Scripture.

The most striking incident of this kind is that of the young ruler. With a hasty tread, and with fitting reverence and deep earnestness, he approaches the Savior and inquired of him for the way to eternal life. And "Jesus beholding him loved him."

How was this possible?

How could Christ love a youth, who was so full of self-righteousness, and so lamentably blind with regard to his true state of heart; who went away sorrowful, when the royal road to eternal life was pointed out to him?

It is sufficiently clear, that the Savior did not approve every trait of this ruler's character. If so, what necessity was there to put him to such a severe test, which made him see himself in the true light. There was one particular quality which our Lord greatly admired in this young man, and it was this very same quality, which in general was lacking among the youth of his time, viz: *honest striving* after the better life.

In our daily contact with men, we often come across those, in whom we find certain virtues or graces, which lead us to admire them, even in spite of their numerous defects and immoralities. Scholars often speak with warm enthusiasm about certain passages which they find in infidel writers, while they have no sympathy whatever with their views and sentiments.

Have you never heard men admire the ingenuity and dexterity of the successful robber or juggler whose base acts they abhorred?

This is the case in our text. Our Lord's eye is fastened on a single point, excluding all others.

It is the *prudent foresight*, not the *dishonest policy*, which Jesus commends in the parable of which these words constitute a part. Let us briefly glance at this parable, in order that we may the better understand the passage under consideration.

The Great Teacher—who spake as never man spake—portrays here a true child of the world. The picture is neither unusual nor overdrawn. The history of our own country, during these past years, has afforded us the most striking proofs of this.

An unscrupulous steward is here brought to our notice, who has the oversight and management of all his Lord's kingly possessions. These seem to consist mainly of landed estate, and are rented to tenants, who pay a certain proportion of the crop, which would naturally vary according to the harvest.

The oriental steward, unlike those of modern times, w required annually to give a complete account of all the income, and to consult his lord about all important business transactions. On the contrary, unlimited confidence was placed in him, and he could settle all affairs according to his best judgment. This was more than this conscienceless steward could stand. He managed things in his own interests, regardless of the landlord or of the tenant. He made the poor tenant pay an enormous rate of rent, and made but small returns to the proprietor. The difference between what he received, and what he rendered, was a clear gain to himself. On this he lived sumptuously, quite unconscious of his guilt, and the consequences of his course.

But the sins of men always find them out, though not always in this world.

It was not long before his unsuspecting lord came on the track of his villainous transactions. We can easily imagine his anger, when he realizes how shamefully his confidence has been abused.

The unfaithful steward is summoned to render his account as soon as possible, as he will no longer employ this wretch in his responsible position. This unsuspected calamity arouses him to a startling realization. Presently he will be without employment, and he has not a cent laid up for the evil day. Like all fast men, he has fully lived up to his income, and possibly beyond it. He has been very improvident as well as dishonest. " What shall he do?" " How shall he live?" Is there no way to escape the terrible experience of poverty?

What shall he do when to-morrow he stands under the bare heavens, penniless, friendless and helpless?

As he has always been accustomed to light inside work, he is not able to earn a living by hard outdoor labor, and as he always lived in splendid style, he is ashamed to beg.

How many an unscrupulous clerk or employe throughout our country is continually reduced to the same straits.

Honesty is a much easier road to travel than fraud or trickery. It saves men from these terrible dilemmas.

Honest and industrious men are seldom, if ever, reduced to beggary. Misfortune may befall them, and their vast possessions may be laid in ashes, but their "good name" will survive amid all the crumblings of business and of wealth, and as long as a man has that, he cannot be considered poor.

The steward, spoken of in the parable, after a moment's reflection, has conceived a plan whereby to make provision against that time of need and destitution, which is now so near at hand. "Eureka," I have found it, he exclaims in high glee. The means to which he resorts, in order to save himself in his present emergency, are in perfect consistency with his previous course.

He will make friends of his lord's debtors. He will use these remaining hours of his stewardship to his very best perso vantage. What these past years have not done, these last moments will accomplish.

He will prepare for himself a warm reception in many a home. With the greatest speed possible he calls every one of his lord's debtors, one by one, no doubt. "How much owest thou unto my lord?" is the question he puts to the first. "A hundred measures of oil," is the prompt reply.

"Take thy bill and sit down quickly, and write fifty."

When a second debtor appears before him, he asks the same question, "how much owest thou?" When he tells him a hundred measures of wheat, he says, "take thy bill and write eighty." In this way he dealt with a great many.

It requires no vivid imagination to picture this proceeding, as one after another of these burdened tenants reaped the advantage of this unscrupulous policy. They go back to their homes highly gratified, and their mouths flow over with the praise of a man so generous, and considerate of their toil and poverty. When they afterwards hear of his expulsion from office, it grieves them, and they look upon it as an act of gross injustice. Wherever occasion offers they utter a word in his favor, and when he has lost his remunerative post, they cannot bear to let him suffer, to whom they are under the greatest obligations.

When his lord—not ours—heard of this, he commended the unjust steward; not his unjustice and infidelity, but the prudence and shrewdness with which he acted, in order to escape the evil which threatened him. And our Lord observing this, says: "the children of this world are in their generation *wiser* than the children of light."

It is a *startling fact*, which the Savior here utters. Of course, we are not to apply this truth to all the children of light. There have been noble exceptions. Both Scripture and history prove this. There have been those, who have freely sacrificed this present world for the next. There are those still, who honor God and bless mankind by their consistent, heavenly lives. But the followers of Jesus, alas! are not all of that stamp. There are but too many, who attempt to serve two masters. They are "children of light" in the sense that they know the truth, but how far are they from doing it!

It is at these, that Christ directs his blows. He would have them remember, that it is not enough to bear the beautiful and striking name of " children of light", if they do not walk in the light.

That the Savior had every reason to assert, that the children of the world were wiser in their generation—i. e. in wordly matters—than the children of light in spiritual things, must be conceded at once, when we compare the one with the other.

I. First of all

"The Carefulness Of The Children Of The World, Over Against The Carelessness Of The Children Of Light,

strikes our eye.

The steward has hardly become conscious of the doom, which hangs above his head, when the deepest anxiety fills his soul.

"My lord taketh away the stewardship from me," is the uppermost thought in his mind; and the all-absorbing question of his heart is, "what shall I do?" Not a moment passes but what he ponders over these things. It banishes sleep from his eye-lids, and fills his mind with gloomy thoughts and sad fore-bodings. His countenance, his words, all his bearing plainly indicate great depression of mind. The things, which were most agreeable to him before, have lost all their attraction. The sweetest music produces no happier sensation upon him, than the most hideous discords, and the most palatable dainties he enjoys no better than the coarsest food.

His whole mind is bent on one thing—how he may avoid the terrible fate of being thrown on the mercies of a cold world.

This man is only an illustration of the great body of worldly men. How great is their forethought about the unknown future. What time and thought they devote to their various business transactions. With what shrewdness they contrive, and with what exactness and determination they carry out all their plans.

(5).

How every failure depresses them, as if their very existence were at stake! Now look at the children of light. How much carelessness they manifest in regard to infinitely higher things.

They profess that they are not their own, but the servants of him, whom they acknowledge to be the sole proprietor of the entire Universe. They acknowledge, that they are merely his stewards and are to render him an account of all of property and brains and influence, and opportunity given them. They are assured, that the time of reckoning is at hand. That the hour may strike at any moment. They realize that they have been exceedingly unfaithful to their great trust; that their account will be more faulty, than that of the steward could possibly be. They have wasted their Lord's goods. They have abused his confidence in them. Yet, notwithstanding all this, how careless they seem; how slow in redeeming the time, and in laying a good foundation for the future.

"Verily the children of this world are wiser in their generation than the children of light."

2. Again, *their pre-eminence in prudence comes out, when we compare* their ASSIDUITY with the SPIRITUAL SLUGGISHNESS of the children of light.

We observe this also in the case of the unjust steward before us. What great inventiveness he displayed in the choice of his remedies. Well may our cheeks burn with shame, when we look at his dexterity.

Scarcely has he realized his danger, when he sets himself at work to contrive a plan, which would help him out of his present difficulty; and how quickly he has invented one, the ingenuity of which his own lord could not but admire.

It was effectual, and could not be surpassed by any one.

It secured him his bread and butter, when he lost his enviable position. If this man had lived in our day, he would have been called a sharper or a shrewd fellow.

We marvel continually at the various methods, which men invent to make money, to enlarge their capital, and to prepare for a rainy day, or the infirmity of old age.

We hardly ever enter a business establishment of some impor-

tance, but what our eye will fall upon some wetstone maxims, such as: "Time is money," "A penny saved, is a penny earned."
  Would that Christians were half as familiar with the instructions of the H. S. and practised them as carefully, as the children of the world follow up their business directions. Many of them vie with one another in their eager chase after riches. What jostling and struggling in the great crowd of competitors. More than ordinary tact and ability is required in our day to be a successful business man and to come out ahead.
  What a blessing it would be, if the children of light possessed a little of that energy and enthusiasm, which men waste on temporal objects. How much they might do to glorify their Master and to save men from an impending perdition.
  But alas! how many we find in a state of utter lethargy, and indifference with respect to the most important affairs, that can be presented to their consideration.
  The words of the godly Bernard are but too true: "there are martyrs of the devil, who put to shame the saints of God." They run with more alacrity to death, than thse to life."
  There is a striking story told of one of the Egyptian Eremites, chancing to see a dancing girl he was moved to tears. Being asked the reason he replied: "That she should be at such pains to please men in a sinful vocation; and we in our holy calling use so little diligence to please God."
  Who will dare to assert, that his tears were unreasonable? Brethren, do we not run with altogether too measured a tread, in the race-course of heaven, which demands the utmost exertion of all our powers?
  Oh, how these words of the poet should ever re-echo in our souls:
"Be this my one great business here,
 With holy trembling, holy fear,
 To make my calling sure."

  3. Again, the children of this world are wiser in their generation, than the children of light, *in their promptitude*, over against the *indecision*, and *procrastination* of the others.
  When the steward had laid out his plans, he lost no time, but

went about at once to execute them. He therefore said "write quickly." He felt that his time was short, and that he could not afford to lose one moment.

Whenever he crossed a field he said to himself, "perhaps this is for the last time."

Every time he left his house, he felt that the time was near at hand, when he would leave it, to come back no more.

Every time he went into a tenant's cottage, he felt soon other feet shall cross this threshold. Only the present is mine. What must be done must be done quickly, soon it will be too late. Wisely the stewart acted. He lost no golden opportunities by procrastination. What he resolved he carried out upon the spot. How differently he acted from many a child of light, who knows that his stewardship is drawing to a close, but makes no provision for an eternal future. He discerns what *can* and *ought* to be done, but he fails to take the things seriously to heart. He keeps putting it off till to-morrow.—In the mean while, childhood and manhood pass. Gray hairs are here and there upon him, and he perceiveth it not.

Every setting sun reminds him of the closing day of his life. And what is the solemn darkness of night, but a type and reminder of the darker, longer night, that soon shall overtake him. How many a one around him has he already seen turned out of his home—and he knows, that his turn may be the next.

Again and again the Master has spoken to him in his providence and by his word. "How is it, that I hear such things of you," and has reminded him, that ere long he must give account of his stewardship.

Abundant opportunity has been given him to prepare his account and to save himself from eternal disgrace and poverty.

But alas, he has wasted his allotted time, as much as all other goods entrusted to him.

He has thought of the most trivial things, but not of the eternal mansions. Like an evil servant, he has said in his heart "my lord delayeth his coming," and has given himself up to all manner of dissipation.

O, how bewildered he will be, when his Lord comes in a day,

when he looked not for him, and in an hour, that he was not aware of. Then it will appear to him and others HOW MUCH WISER *the children of this world* have been, *than the children of light.*

II. The most serious question for us to consider is: THE REASON *why the Savior uttered this humiliating fact.*

He must have had a good reason for it. It seems to me, that his object was, first of all, TO PUT *his lukewarm followers to shame.*

These words, although they were uttered in the presence of the Pharisees, and may have been indirectly aimed at them, as appears from the context, were given for the benefit of our Lord's disciples; doubtless to those, who had recently joined his ranks, and were not as active and enthusiastic in the things of the kingdom of heaven, as he would have them be.

But they are as *much applicable to us,* as *they were to them.*

The parable of this genuine child of the world, so accurately drawn, is *justly shaming.*

What a painful thougnt, that the children of this world, who mind earthly things, and are in a state of moral darkness, should excel the children of the kingdom in *carefulness,* in *assiduity,* and in *resoluteness.* These things ought not so to be. The very thought, that we are the children of light, should incite us to earnestness and diligence. What inestimable privileges, but also what great responsibilities are linked with this most precious name? Should not we, who are called to be perfect, even as our Father in heaven is perfect, strive to excel those, who live still in sin, in everything, that is worth excelling in? Or shall the howling owl, which only sees in the dark, excel the eagle, proud bird of the skies, who mounts up on high and bathes himself in the effulgent rays of the sun?

How much superior our interests are to those of the men of the world. *They* build below the skies, and their plans do not extend beyond the confines of time. They throw their utmost powers on things of earth, on a scheme perhaps, which breaks up like a cloud-phantom, or melts away like an ice-palace—while we seek enduring treasures in heaven, and reach forward, not to secure an earthly habitation, but a "building not made with hands, eternal in the heavens." Now if these inferior things, which the children of this world pursue—are in their estimation worthy of such devoted earnestness and persevering efforts, how much more the eternal things!........

2. Another reason, why Jesus spoke these words, was to *arouse his followers* to the full extent of all their powers. This appears from the words with which he closes this beautiful parable.

And I say unto you, "Make to yourselves friends of the Mammon of unrighteousness; that, when ye fail, they may receive you into everlasting habitations. He, that is faithful in that which is least, is faithful also in much; and he that is unjust in the least is unjust also in much. If, therefore, ye have not been faithful in the unrighteous Mammon, who will commit to your trust the *true* riches? And if ye have not been faithful in that which is another man's, who shall give you that which is your own?"

Our Lord would have his disciples put every talent, entrusted fo them, to usury.

Therefore he exhorts them to make themselves friends out of the "Mammon of unrighteousness."

Mammon is the name of a Syrian god, who presided over wealth. This god is here called "UNRIGHTEOUS," because wealth is frequently used not well but ill. Its tendency is to corrupt and harden men. Hence these repeated admonitions in Scripture against it. By Mammon, we are not necessarily to understand gold or silver, but any wealth; wealth meaning weal or well-being. Our wealth, or well-being may consist in money, honor, influence or power. In a word, every thing that we possess and that is valuable to us, is wealth, and may become our Mammon.

"To make friends of him," is to convert him into an ally, or in other words, to use these temporal advantages in such a way, that we shall thereby advance our spiritual interests.

The Savior in these words alludes to the unjust steward, who acted shrewdly in making friends out of his master's goods.

He would have us act in the same manner, and have us secure

friends in heaven by our holy and unselfish deeds, so that, whenever we shall fail and be removed from our stewardship by death, those, whom we have made our friends by our charitable assistance, will receive us into everlasting habitations.

"Not"—to quote the words of a popular commentator, "that this will in any measure merit that blessed recompense, or that the poor, whom he has relieved, can have the disposal of it; or that all, whom he has relieved, were pious persons or all removed to heaven," but as the cries of the oppressed and neglected poor will testify to unfaithful stewards to their condemnation, so the prayers of widows and orphans for their pious benefactors will testify for them, that they were faithful; and such believers, as have died before them, may be considered as standing ready to welcome their benefactors to their everlasting habitations, when they quit the earth."

The truth, that by earthly wealth we may secure to us heavenly possessions, is beautifully illustrated by a legend of the apostle Thomas. It is related that the Lord appeared to him in Cæsarea and informed him, that Gondaphorus, king of the Indies, wished a finer palace, than that of the Emperor of Rome.

At the Lord's bidding he went to the Indies, and king Gondaphorus gave him a large amount of silver and gold, and commanded him to build therewith a magnificent palace. The king went away for two years. On his return he found that St. Thomas had given away all the gold and silver to the poor and sick. He was angry and cast him into a prison, preparatory to inflicting a horrible death. In the mean time the king's brother died; but in four days he rose, and told king Gondaphorus, that he must not harm St. Thomas, "for," said he, "I have been to Paradise, and the angels showed me a wondrous palace of gold and silver and precious stones, and said 'This is the palace which St. Thomas has builded for thy brother Gondaphorus'."

But as the great majority of Christ's disciples were then, and still are, comparatively poor, they might be inclined to think that this exhortation did not apply to them. Hence Jesus adds: "He that is faithful in that which is least, is faithful also in much, and he that is unjust in the least, is unjust also in much."

Alas! how often men forget these words;—how many lose out of sight that God is trying our fidelity every day and every hour.

Oh, how much depends upon these few brief years, upon these few earthly talents! The *true* riches, those treasures, which are satisfying and enduring will never be entrusted to him, who has not been faithful in the unrighteous Mammon.

If any one is unfaithful in the things entrusted to him for a time, and of which he must speedily render an account, how can he expect the Lord to give him at last an inheritance to be his own by an inalienable tenure. What earthly lord could give an estate to his servant, when he had been all along dishonest and unfaithful in the trust reposed in him. How then can we expect that God will make us heirs of the eternal treasures, and inhabitants of the glorious mansions prepared by Christ for his faithful ones.

Oh how many deceive themselves on this point. They do not realize, that the life beyond is the ripe fruit of life below.

Many seem to think, that we may live and act as we will, provided our lives be moral. This is a fatal mistake! We are not our own. We are Christ's, as he is God's. He keeps a close eye on every talent, which he has committed to our trust. Our all depends upon a proper use of them. In view of this, how awfully solemn is life. "What manner of persons ought we to be in all holy conversation and godliness."

We should, if possible, be even more prudent, than the children of this world. Our whole lives should bear the distinct marks of decision, earnestness, and consecration. Without strong determination and energy, no earthly wealth can be amassed; much less these *true* riches.

It is for this reason that Scripture enjoins us to lay hold of eternal life, to strive to enter in through the narrow gate.

All our temporal concerns must be viewed by us as secondary, and we must be willing to surrender, if necessary, everything, which is dear to us on earth, in order that we may secure the blessings of salvation.

Once on a time a vessel, freighted with gold, was wrecked

under circumstances, which left her crew no chance of life, but swimming to the distant shore. Some had committed themselves to the deep; others were stripping for the struggle, when one, turning an avaricious eye on the treasures, seized the fortune at his hand. Infatuated wretch! His fellows remonstrated, but in vain. Loaded with gold he leaps from the ship, and strikes out bravely for the shore. But by-and-bye his strokes grew feebler, quicker—then a short convulsive struggle—and then, borne down by the weight he carries, he sinks beneath the waves. You call this man a fool, and you say that you would not have acted his part, if you had been in the same circumstances. We gladly believe this. But are you not guilty of infinitely greater folly, if you allow yourself to be engrossed with the pursuits of time, whether of business or pleasure, to the neglect of your salvation?

"What does it profit a man, if he gain the whole world, and lose his own soul."

Therefore, "think of the home over there." This earthly tabernacle of yours will soon give way. Already it is wearing out and yielding to the rude storms of life. Before you are aware of it, it will come down with sudden crash. Make haste therefore to be wise. Amend the past, and seize the present. Confess your past unfaithfulness to your Redeemer; and henceforth seek with a purpose of heart the kingdom of God, and its righteousness, and when heart and flesh shall fail, he will receive you to glory. Then in the words of the poet

> "Out of your last home dark and cold
> Thou shalt pass to a city whose streets are gold;
> From the silence that falls upon sin and pain,
> To the deathless joys of the angel's strain;
> Well shall be ended what ill began
> Out of the shadow into the sun."

The Apostasy of Demas.

> For Demas hath forsaken me, having loved
> the present world. 2 Tim. 4:10.

WHEN the apostle wrote these painful words to Timothy, his much beloved son in the Gospel, he was all but happily situated.

We find him in the dark and chilly dungeon in the city of Rome, patiently waiting for the verdict, that shall deliver him to the cruel sword of the Roman executioner. But he was ready to be offered. In full consciousness, that his life-work was finished, and that a most glorious reward was in store for him—he says: "I have fought a good fight, I have finished my course, I have kept the faith; henceforth there is laid up for me a crown of righteousness, which the Lord, the righteous judge, shall give me at that day; and not to me only, but unto all them, that love his appearing."

In these trying hours, he has learned by sad experience how little human friendship is to be relied upon. When he, more than ever, needed a word of sympathy or a look of encouragement, he found it not.

"At my first answer no man stood with me, but all men forsook me." Like the Master in the night of his betrayal, all his companions, stricken by panic, had deserted him. One had fled in haste to Thessalonica, another to Galatia, another to Dalmatia. He was left all alone—and yet not alone, for when he was summoned at Nero's bar, the Lord stood with him, and strengthened him, and he was delivered out of the mouth of the lion.

This unkind and undeserved treatment, which Paul received at the hands of his friends, did not lead him to indulge in angry feeling against them; for he writes "I pray God, that it may not be laid to their charge." Still, in the manner in which he speaks of it, we distinctly detect a tone of sadness.

What has grieved him most of all—is the departure of Demas, who has forsaken him from love to the present world. There was a vast difference between *his* departure and *that* of the other brethren. "They," as some one has rightly remarked, "fled the field for a time, he forever; they abandoned the fight, he the faith; their conduct was a weakness, his was apostasy; theirs the failing of the disciples for whom their Master offered the kind apology—"the spirit indeed is willing, but the flesh is weak;"—but his the crime and guilt of Judas."

The name and crime of this man have been recorded in these imperishable pages as a warning to professors of religion in all future ages. And who can think of this brilliant light going out in utter darkness, without holy trembling, and without saying to himself "truly let him, that standeth, take heed lest he fall."

I. Let us briefly gather the light, which Scripture casts upon the history of this once great man.

We know but very little of Demas. Some infer, that his home was at Thessalonica from the fact, that he started for that place, when he forsook the apostle at his awful crisis at Rome.

We are not informed of him, as we are of Timothy, that he had a pious ancestry and knew the Holy Scriptures from a child. Nor are we told what his previous life and character had been, or how and where he embraced christianity. But we know from the confidence Paul placed in him, and from the love, which he seems to have cherished for him, *that he had made a good profession.*

He had, for a time at least, given up the world, and had consecrated himself to the service of Jesus Christ. He had laid his hand on the plough. He had prepared himself for the Christian race. He did run well. He was sound in doctrine, virtuous in practice.

He occupied a prominent position in the Church. The apostle Paul, who stood head and shoulder above all the other brethren, and whose praise was in all the churches, had not only deemed him worthy of his warmest affection, but had also selected him as a fellow-laborer in the Lord.

From this we may safely infer, that he had more than ordinary talents, and was in human judgment "a man full of the faith and of the Holy Ghost."

The apostle makes honorable mention of him in his pastoral letters—which proves that he was known and beloved in the Churches.

In his letter to the Colossians he associated his name with one of the four Evangelists--"Luke", says he, "the beloved physician, and *Demas* greet you." Again, in his touching epistle to Philemon, we find his name introduced in no less honorable company, "There salute thee," he says "Epaphras, my fellow-prisoner in Christ Jesus, Marcus, Aristarchus, Demas, Luke, my fellow-laborers. What a galaxy of stars, and Demas shining among them! Surely, he must have been a great man.

Who can tell, how useful he has been, what trophies he may have won for the Christian religion. How many sinners by his instrumentality have been brought to the Savior's feet. How many brethren by his timely word and bright example have been strengthened and braced up in the Christian warfare.

Who knows what precious words of comfort he has spoken, and what solemn words of warning have often trembled on his lips. To the contrite he has been a Barnabas, a son of consolation; and to the proud sinner a Boanerges—a son of thunder.

Not only has he *preached* the Gospel, but he has also *suffered* for it—for Paul not merely speaks of him as a fellow-laborer, but also as a fellow-prisoner.

> "Alas! that even the martyr's cell,
> Heaven's very gates, should scope allow
> For the false world's seducing spell."

Alas, tnat he looked back. How sad that such a man should fall. Were he a private soldier in the blessed Savior's cause, we should not have thought so much of it, to see him desert the ranks and quit the field;—but that the martyr should become a renegade, the brave soldier a miserable deserter, the general a traitor, must strike the Christian heart with sorrow and dismay.

What a gloomy picture our text presents of this once brave and useful man.

Had Paul written no second letter to Timothy, or if God in his wise providence had seen fit to keep this epistle from the Church at large, as many other writings from the same pen, we could not but have thought highly of him, and his name would doubtles, even to this day, have been prominent among the saints in the Romish calendar.

But he has not only, like some, outlived his usefulness, but also his honor and principles.

Happy would it have been for him, if his sun had gone down at noon.

In that case, his name would have lived on forever in hallowed recollection. And above his grave, where the apostle has now carved in indelible characters this awful epitaph—"Demas hath forsaken me, having loved the present world," the Church of all ages would have these comforting words: "Blessed are the dead, which die in the Lord from henceforth; yea, saith the spirit, that they may rest from their labors; and their works do follow them."

What became of Demas from the hour in which he deserted the apostle, Scripture does not say. When he becomes disloyal to the cause he once with heart and hand advanced, he is no longer worthy of its notice.

If ancient tradition gives us a true account, he went from bad to worse, sank lower and lower, from one depth of wickedness to another, till he closed his infamous career, as a priest of a heathen temple, offering sacrifices to dead stocks and stones.

Demas deserves justly to be called the Balaam of the New Testament. Like him, he had from the lofty eminence he once occupied, poured forth the most sacred benedictions upon the head of the people of God, and lent his help to forward their cause.

Like him, he had seen the most glorious prospects, which were opened up before them, and had given utterance to the desire "let me die the death of the righteous, and let my last end be like his."

Like him, he perished on the battle-field, as a bitter opponent of God and his people; giving the Church and the world a most striking proof, that a good beginning may yet have a terrible end.

II. BUT WHAT WAS THE CAUSE OF SO TERRIBLE A FALL?

The apostle tells us, that it was LOVE TO THIS PRESENT WORLD.

Great effects may often be traced back to small, almost insignificant causes.

A returned missionary from India, when speaking in London of the condition of heathenism in his field of labor, said, that during the past year the city of Puri was thrown into great consternation on account of the falling of a stone from the roof of Juggernaut's temple, which was erected some seven hundred years ago, and on which, from that time, there had not been a trowel laid for repairs.

After the falling of this stone, which weighed some ten or twelve tons, the building was examined and it was found to be entirely unsafe and on the verge of ruin.

Now what was the cause of this sudden dilapidation? There was no mystery about it. The birds had carried berries from the Banyantree to the top of the building and had dropped the seeds, when they fell into the crevices between the stones, and there, buried in the dust of ages, when watered by the dews of heaven and warmed by the sunbeams, these seeds had germinated and the tiny roots had struck down among the stones, working their way hither and thither, until, like powerful levers, they had heaved the massive rocks and separated one from another the ponderous stones, which composed this magnificent structure.

Now as a few small insignificant seeds may shatter and bring destruction upon such a grand edifice, built by the wealth of ages, and the toils of generations, which had stood firm through successive centuries—so a few little sins, yea even one, may gradually bring ruin upon the finest moral structure, which the world has ever seen.

It was no great crime, which Demas had committed, no heinous sin, which worked out his distruction.

It was only *love to the present world.* When he had enlisted in the service of Christ, he had given up many a sin, many a forbidden pleasure, many an earthly treasure; but there were some heart-strings, which fastened him to the world, which were not snapped. There was one idol at least, which was not expelled from the throne of his heart—one sin, to which he persistently held on. He had forgotten those solemn words of Jesus "Whosoever he be of you, that forsaketh not ALL, that he hath, he cannot be my disciple."

He had not made a full surrender of himself—though it seemed so to all human appearance. He evidently made a very fair show of his Christian profession, else the apostle Paul would not have chosen him as a fellow-laborer.

But the best of human judges is liable to be deceived.

Demas, though he may have appeared like a fruitful tree planted by rivers of water, yielded nothing but leaves.

The root of the matter was not in him. In the hidden depth of his soul—he still *loved the present world.*

There this *love*, like the tiny seed, lay slumbering; fed by indulgence, it grew—so silently perhaps, that while it was worming itself deeper in, and wrapping its strong roots round and round his heart, he never for one moment suspected the hold it was taking upon him.

Like the devotees of juggernaut, he became conscious of his condition, when it was too late, when the whole fabric of his character was undermined by this love of the world.

Demas was one of that class of Gospel hearers, whose state of heart our Lord compares to stony places, where the seed of the word had no deepness of earth, and forthwith sprung up, but was scorched, when the sun arose, and because it had no root withered away.

This disciple was all right as long as it was smooth sailing, when no adverse winds beat upon him; but when tribulation or persecution arose, because of the word, he became offended.

He held out well, until it actually came to a choice between God and the world.

When from his love to the Savior he was required to yield worldly care, home comforts, earthly treasures—yea perhaps his very life, he denied his Master, and forsook the apostle.

Poor Demas has a thousand fears. He fears poverty, the prison, the scaffold, death. All because he lacks that perfect love, which casteth out all fear. All because he cannot say from the heart "Whom have I in heaven but thee? and there is none upon the earth that I desire besides thee? My flesh and my heart faileth, but God is the strength of my heart and my portion forever."

Love to this present world! Is not this, my friends, the fatal rock on which thousands have suffered shipwreck?

How many we find in sacred record, who have been caught in this terrible snare of the great enemy. It has been the ruin of Balaam, a prophet of Jehovah; of Achan a most prominent man among the children of Israel; of Gehazi the servant of the godly Elisha.

It led Judas to betray his Master—Ananias and Sapphira to lie against the Holy Ghost. It prevented the young ruler from entering the kingdom of heaven, and Demas from pressing forward to the crown. Against nothing are we so seriously warned in Holy Writ.

God does not forbid his children to enjoy the good things of this world.

Does he not freely and bountifully bestow them upon us? Has he not purchased them for us by the blood of his Son? And does not the apostle emphatically tell us "every creature of God is good and nothing to be refused, if it be received with thanksgiving; for it is sanctified by the word of God and prayer?" Still, we are commanded not to set our affections on these things, not to make them the supreme object of our desires.

The Savior himself has said: "Children how hard is it for them, that trust in riches, to enter into the kingdom of heaven. It is easier for a camel to go through the eye of a needle"—the smallest conceivable hole—"than for a rich man"—i. e. one, who trusts in riches—" to enter into the kingdom of heaven."

The world is God's rival, and the room we make for it in our hearts cannot be occupied at the same time by God, whom we are called to love with our whole being.

It is this which the Savior endeavored to inculcate, when he so earnestly said: " No man can serve two masters, for either he will hate the one and love the other, or hold to the one and despise the other—ye cannot serve God and mammon."

It is this, which led the apostle James to exclaim, "Ye adulterers and adulteresses, know ye not that the friendship of the world is emnity to God? whosoever, therefore, will be a friend of the world, is the enemy of God." And John has testified—" if any man love the world, the love of the Father is not in him."

III.

AN APOSTASY LIKE THAT OF DEMAS, COULD NOT BUT PRODUCE THE MOST DISASTROUS CONSEQUENCES.

Let us briefly note a few. It was a most painful blow to the apostle himself in this trying hour to see a man, so prominent and useful, desert him, especially in such a cowardly manner. How wholly contrary this was to his own noble spirit. There was nothing in the world, that could induce him to forsake the cause of Christianity—for he was under constraint—"the love of Christ constrained him." This wonderful love, which surpasseth knowledge, exercised its omnipotent power over him.

It enabled him to do and to bear, to any and to every extent. What must have grieved this faithful servant most was the fact, that this desertion weakened his Master's cause. He knew how the enemies of the cross would glory in this. They would say— "don't you see these Christians are only blind enthusiasts. They give up when it becomes too hot for them. There is Demas, one of the foremost of them—he has run off, and come back to our side again. What cowards these Christians are. This excitement will not last. If their religion was, what they pretended it to be, they would stand by it till the last. They would not be so anxious to give it up, when they see it is going to cost them something. Who will join their ranks, if their own leaders quit the field.

This desertion must also have had a *weakening effect on the Church itself.* Did we say a moment ago that it was a blow to Paul, it was this to every member of the Church.

How it must have saddened the heart of Timothy and the Church at Ephesus, when this letter of Paul reached them, and they read concerning this brother, whom many knew, and of whose labors they had heard so much—" Demas hath forsaken me, having loved the present world."

What bad news this was! Who will be the next, they must have asked; *Lord is it I—is it I?*

But we can conceive how God, who causeth all things to work together for good to them, that love him, could even make the fall of this man productive to the establishment of his people in the faith. It was a terrible warning, which could not remain without the most wholesome effects. How many, that slept in Zion, it aroused from their slumbers. How many it led to the most careful examination of heart.

It taught the Church to pray not only for themselves, but also for their leaders, and to "exhort one another daily, while it is called to-day, lest any be hardened through the deceitfulness of sin."

It taught the highest to give heed, lest he fall; the happiest to rejoice with trembling; and each one to watch and pray, lest he enter into temptation.

The effects of this going back to the world, *must have been sad in the extreme upon the apostate himself.* Never in his life had he taken such a fatal step. Better a thousand times would it have been for that man, if he had not been born, than, like another Judas, to betray his Master—because he loved the present world. How much better off is Paul in his lonely prison-cell, without a cheering word, or friendly smile, than Demas surrounded with all the attractions and enjoyments of a present world.

Has he enjoyed peace at Thessalonica? Has the present world made up to him for the eternal loss, which she had inflicted on his immortal soul? How did he feel when the present world left him, and the bloody apparition of the martyred apostle, whom he had forsaken—haunted him on his death bed?

* * * * * * *

Many instructive lessons may be gathered from the apostasy of this disciple.

1. His history calls on us, first of all, TO PUT NO TRUST IN MAN. We are very apt to do this,—and if we do, we will be sure to deceive ourselves. It is on this account, that the great apostle exhorts us, not to build our faith on man; for the most exalted in the kingdom of heaven is liable to fall; the most dazzling of human lights may go out in endless night. There is but one foundation, one chief corner-stone, on which we can safely build our hopes for heaven. It is the Lord Jesus Christ. We may rejoice in the good and the brave, who adorn the Christian religion. We cannot appreciate too much the zeal and ability of a Paul, and the eloquence of an Apollos, but we may not idolize them. If we do this, we shall suffer the consequences. When the lofty oak is hurled down by the sweeping storm, the ivy, which clings to his branches, is humiliated with him.

Happy the man, therefore, who trusts in the Lord, for he shall be like Mount Zion, which shall not be moved!

2. We learn from this history also, that NO SPIRITUAL ATTAINMENTS OR RELIGIOUS ADVANTAGES ARE SUFFICIENT TO WARRANT US AGAINST THE MOST TERRIBLE FALL. To what spiritual height Demas had attained. How pure the moral atmosphere he breathed. He could have had no better companions on this side of heaven.

He could have had no more elevating work.—All his surroundings seemed to have been favorable to the upbuilding of his Christian character. He was in circumstances less likely than any of us to get engrossed with the business alone, or burdened with the cares, or entangled with the pleasures, of the world. Notwithstanding, he fell—drawn away by the love of the world from the love of Christ.

What need, then, for us to watch and pray, and to guard with all diligence the state of our hearts.

What need, then, to be clothed with humility, and to walk in holy fear, all the days of our earthly pilgrimage.

> 'Tis sad—but yet 'tis well, be sure,
> We on the sight should muse awhile,
> Nor deem our shelter all secure,
> Even in the Church's holiest aisle.
> Vainly before the shrine he bends,
> Who knows not the true pilgrim's part;
> The martyr's cell no safety lends,
> To him, who wants the martyr's heart.

3. Lastly, we are here most solemnly admonished AGAINST LOVING THE WORLD. Who would have thought, that this remaining spark of worldly love—in the breast of Demas, would have resulted in such fearful destruction. But you say "we are not exposed to such persecutions as seem to have led to his fall." This may all be true, but don't you know, that the world has trials more testing and severe than these?

Its smiles are much more to be dreaded than its frowns; its subtle sophistry works out more harm, than the sharpest sword. Oh, how this love of the present world is damaging the Church of Christ in our day. It paralyzes all Christian energy, and undermines all philanthropic efforts. Where is that burning zeal for Christ—where that spirit of self-sacrifice—where that unbounded liberality, that holy joy, that grand enthusiasm for the salvation of men, that so characteristically marked the apostolic days?

What has extinguished this holy fire? Is it not love to the present world? Has not this dreadful disease crippled and disfigured many a Church?

How many a Christian society, which once might be compared to the noble Church of Smyrna or Philadelphia, has come to resemble lukewarm Laodicea, or like Sardis merely lives in name, while in reality it is dead! May not that terrible word "Ichabod" —"thy glory has departed"—be written over many a once spiritually growing Church? When we come to examine our lists of membership—behind how many a name must be written—"hath forsaken us, having loved the present world!"

And of those, who still remain true to their Church obligations, how many are continually looking back to the world—and, if weighed in the balances of the sanctuary, are found sadly wanting?

How timely are the remarks of the learned MacKay in his little work entitled " Grace and Truth."

In this land, at this moment, it is difficult to know the *Church* from the *world*. The world, "of the earth earthy," has said to the Church, the bride of the Lamb, "of the heavens heavenly," come a little down to us, and we will rise a little up to you, and we can shake hands and agree. This, in the present day, is called LIBERALITY, CHARITY, LARGE-HEARTEDNESS, and he who dares to dissent is called a bigot, one of peculiar views, a man of extremes.

The world makes its social gathering and invites the Christian. A compromise is effected. The Christian leaves at home his peculiar testimony for his rejected Lord.

The world lays aside a little of its open worldliness, and they thus agree. The world has been raised somewhat. Its tone has been elevated. The Christian has come down from his high standing-ground, and has lost his place as the separated one. His Lord is dishonored, and this is modern liberality! The world and the Christian agree, and God's name, God's glory, the offense of the cross, are given up as the price of the agreement.

In olden times, among the stories of the sea, the superstitious sailors used to relate one of a strange island, that lay in waters, where no breakers beat, nor storms blew on its quiet shores. This island was the dread of mariners. They feared it even more, than the most treacherous rocks and shoals. Being composed of a mass of magnetic ore, it had the most singular powers of attraction. When the ship had once come within the reach of its influence, it was *gone*.

There was no possibility of escape. The most desperate efforts were all in vain. The ship was drawn nearer and nearer—at first slowly, silently, gently, almost imperceptibly—but with ever increasing speed—till, on a close approach, every iron bolt drawn from her timbers, without a crash or sound, or anything to alarm the waking, or to arouse the sleeping, she fell into a thousand pieces, and, the whole fabric dissolved, crew and cargo sank together—down into that quiet sea.

In vain we traverse earth's seas to discover this beautiful, but treacherous isle. But though we do not find it in the *natural*, we find something equal to it in the *moral* world.

Worldliness, is the magnetic rock, which stands athwart the Christian's path.

Its attraction is subtle, silent, slow, but fearfully powerful on every soul, that floats within its range. "Under its enchanting spell," says Dr. Cuyler, "bolt after bolt of good resolution, clamp after clamp of Christian obligation, are stealthily drawn out. What matters it how long or how fair has been the man's profession of religion; or how flauntingly the flag of his orthodoxy floats from the headmast. Let sudden temptation smite the unbolted professor, and in an hour he is a wreck." We cannot too seriously warn you against this mighty loadstone of attraction, which has already ruined so many a Demas. If you find yourself beginning to love any pleasure better than your prayers—any book better than your Bible—any evening entertainment, better than your prayer-meeting—any person better than your Savior—a present indulgence better, than the hopes of heaven—let me sound the signal of alarm.

You are in danger. You are within the range of the fatal magnetic rock.

Flatter not yourself with the idea, that this beginning of sin is so small. Only a small leak causes the ship to sink and drowns her precious crew. Behold how great a matter a little fire kindleth!

How necessary, therefore, that we in all seriousness give heed to the exhortation "Love not the world, neither the things, that are in the world. If any man love the world, the love of the Father is not in him. For all that is in the world, the lust of the flesh, and the lust of the eyes, and the pride of life, is not of the Father, but is of the world. And the world passeth away, and the lust thereof; but he, that doeth the will of God, abideth for ever."

Think not, my friends, that the Bible means to have us become hermits, or wants us to shut ourselves up in monasteries. This would be as much a sin, as it is to mingle with the world. No, we may enjoy the rich bounties, which the kind Creator has so lavishly provided for us,—but we may not make these the great end of our living. The world is very good, if kept in its own place.

Like the elements of nature, it is a useful servant, but a bad and most tyrannical master. There is even a sense in *which we may love* the world, and cannot love it too fervently. We may love it with the love of him, who gave his only begotten Son to die for it. We may love it, with the love of him, who shed his blood to save it. We may love it, with the love of angels, who rejoice in its conversion. We may love it, so as to do it good. We may give our tears to its sufferings—our pity to its sorrows—our wealth to its wants—our prayers to its miseries—our time and powers to its advancement in virtue and real godliness.

But this is is the world of mankind........

Remember that your Savior calls you the light of the world; the salt of the earth. Either, you must have an influence upon it for good, or it will certainly have an influence upon you for evil. Never forget this apostolic admonition—let it be inscribed upon the walls of our homes, and upon the tablets of our hearts—"Be not *conformed* to this world; but be ye *transformed* by the renewing of your mind, that ye may prove what is that good, and acceptable and perfect will of God."

Do you ask me for a preventive against loving the world? I know but one. It is the love of the Father—study it, believe it. Let it fill your mind and heart, and there will no longer be room for an empty, vanishing world. Then you will say with the poet—

> "Give what thou wilt, without thee we are poor,
> And with thee rich, take what thou wilt away!"

No prayer, therefore, can be more appropriate for every follower of Christ, than this, which the apostle Paul offered for the Ephesian Church.

"I bow my knees unto the Father of our Lord Jesus Christ ....that he would grant you according to the riches of his glory ....that Christ may dwell in your hearts by faith; that ye being rooted and grounded in love, may be able to comprehend with all saints what is the breadth and length, and height; and to know the love of Christ, which passeth knowledge, that ye might be filled with all the fulness of God."

* * * * * * *

And when you see other disciples go back to the world, and walk no more with the Master, and the testing question is put to you: "Will ye also go away?"—You will reply in heartfelt enthusiasm—"Lord, to whom shall we go? Thou hast the words of eternal life."

Double Prosperity.

> "Beloved, I wish above all things that those mayest prosper and be in health, even as thy soul prospereth."
>
> 3 John 2.

 UR text forms the introduction of the shortest Epistle in the whole Bible.

It was directed to a private Christian, named Gaius.

Who this individual was we cannot tell, as we read of a great many by that name.

The most plausible supposition is that he was a convert of St. John, and a layman of wealth and distinction, residing in some city near Ephesus.

The object of this brief Epistle seems to be, to recommend to the kindness and hospitality of Gaius some Christians, who were strangers in the place of his residence. It appears from the letter itself, that the object of these travellers, bearing this note of introduction from an apostolic pen, was to preach the Gospel to the Gentiles, without receiving temporal support from them.

St. John had previously written to the ecclesiastical authorities of the place, recommending these men to their care, and love, but they had refused to receive them. This was owing to the instigation of a certain Diotrephes, a leading Presbyter, who held Judaizing views, and would not give assistance to men, who were going about with the purpose of preaching solely to Gentiles.

The apostle, therefore, turns with his modest request to his friend and brother Gaius, and urges him to a compliance with it in these words—"Beloved, follow not that which is evil, but that which is good. He that doeth good is of God; but he that doeth evil hath not seen God."

But it is not our present object to enter into the details of this fraternal letter, although it might be edifying to consider its noble aims and highly Christian spirit. Still, we desire to confine your present attention merely to the introductory sentence. "Beloved, I wish above all things that thou mayest prosper and be in health, even as thy soul prospereth."

. It must be admitted, that there is nothing so very peculiar in this introductory sentence of this friendly letter. It begins very much as every letter begins, with some wish or statement in regard to health. Possibly some may find fault with this introduction, and may have expected to hear something more spiritual from an apostolic pen; but yet what enjoyment could Gaius have tasted of 'grace and peace,' had sickness of body and soul made him incapable of it?

Our text suggests some valuable truths, which are worthy of our most serious consideration.

" Beloved, I wish above all things, that thou mayest prosper and be in health, even as thy soul prospereth."

1. This language of the apostle to his friend implies, *that health and prosperity* are VERY UNCERTAIN.

If this were not the case, this wish would be entirely superfluous. It is not at all necessary to suppose with certain divines, that Gaius was an invalid, or had a weak constitution. Why should immediate sickness be necessary to give utterance to a similar wish? Does not our daily experience justify this? What is more uncertain than health?—We may be uncertain of our possessions, which a single spark reduces to ashes: of our reputation, which a single slanderer may destroy. Yet we are a thousand times more uncertain in regard to our health. Melancholy, yet truthful is Moses' description of human life. He compares it to the flower of the field, which in the morning flourisheth, but in the evening is cut down an withereth. No epidemic need rage in the city, in which Gaius resides, in order to lay him prostrate on a couch of sickness. No "pestilence, that walketh in darkness, no destruction, that wasteth at noonday," need pass from home to home in the place of this discipel's residence, and slay its thousands and ten thousands on the right and on the left of him, to endanger his head, or to deprive him of health.

A single accident, a little malaria in the atmosphere, a sudden fever, a chill, a cold, is all that is needed to bring paleness to his rosy cheeks, weakness to his powerful arm, and pain throughout every joint and fibre of his body. Nothing more than this is needed to rob him of all the joys of life, and make him long for death, and "dig for it, more than for hid treasures."

Gaius might be strong and healthy, when the brethren recently left him, and brought his cummunication to John.

Still the apostle realizes how much may have happened since that parting hour, and even though he be well to-day, before this letter reaches him he may be reclining on a bed of sickness, or death may have cut him off. Hence the apostle begins this hasty fugitive epistle with these words: " Beloved, I wish above all things, that thou mayest prosper, and be in health, even as thy soul prospereth."

With what countless hosts of diseases we are continually surrounded. How delicate and frail is our physical constitution. It is no wonder, that we have so many days of sickness, but it is surprising indeed, that this harp of a thousand strings should be in tune so long.

That we ask one another as often as we meet, in the language of the prophet addressed to the Shunamite—" Is it well with thee? is it well with thy husband? is it well with thy child?" has its touching ground in our saddest experiences.

Alas! that we so often ask this question thoughtlessly and from formality, rather than from deep interest! When we put this question to our friends or acquaintances, we mean to say, that it might not be well with them; that it would not have been surprising to us, if it had not been well with them. The precious gift of health, like so many other blessings, which God so kindly bestows, many pass by without grateful acknowledgement. O, how little yonder rash youth, in whose eye sparkles the love of life, or yonder charming maiden, upon whose cheeks the roses blossom, realize, that the frail summer flower, or the dropping autumn leaf is the image of their existence.

How little is this valueless treasure of health prized by parents, whose dwelling day by day resounds with the merry song and play of their healthful children. Ah, how little is required to change this dwelling into a hospital or a house of mourning. A solitary night, a single hour, a few moments may bring this about.

Oh friends, if we rightly realized how uncertain life and health are, a greater feeling of dependence upon God would fill our souls, and each hour would be more gratefully received, and be more profitably spent. This recklessness, as if there was no end to life and health, would cease. Things which ought to be done to-day would be no longer postponed till to-morrow; and the prayer of the pious Moses would daily flow from our lips with an ever increasing earnestness: "So teach us to number our days, that we may apply our hearts unto wisdom."

2. But it is not only the *uncertainty* of health, which this fervent wish of the apostle for his friend implies, it teaches us also what a *valuable treasure* health is. Beloved, I wish or pray *above all things* that thou mayest prosper and be in health." St. John, as a warm freind of the pious Gaius, wishes him above every other blessing bodily prosperity. Although he wishes him reasonable success in business and a comfortable competency for his declining years, yet what stands out most prominently is the prayer, that he may have *physical health*. This is a blessing of vast importance. To realize this we need only be deprived of it for a few days or hours. Life cannot be enjoyed without it. What are riches, honors, pleasures, knowledge, without the possession of this treasure. The splendour of wealth cannot charm the eye, and the sweetest notes of joy sound like hideous discords to one afflicted with disease. Better, infinitely better, is it to dwell in the humblest hovel, in possession of a strong and healthy body, than to lie down on a princely couch with pain in every limb. Every one, therefore, can appreciate this prayer of Christ's dearest disciple, for his friend Gaius. No, very few

men indeed are so foolish as to desire wealth, honor, or knowledge, in preterence to health. If they do, they know not what they ask. But it is not *merely as a man*, that John asks this blessing for his friend. He desires it much more for him *as a Christian*. If the enjoyment of health is a desirable gift to all, it is this especially to the Christian. He, in the pursuit, of his Heavenly calling, needs it more than any one else. The venerable apostle looked at this matter quite differently from some fanatics of later times, who were so exclusively spiritual, that they despised and neglected the body, in order to devote themselves unreservedly to higher interests. Not so would he have the body, this physical organism of ours, treated. He knows by his own experience how closely body and spirit are associated, and how the condition of the former may impede the latter in pluming its wings for flight.

The Christian should be in every sense the happiest man on earth. Cheerfulness, and contentment should characterize every part of his life, but how is this possible when disease is undermining his entire physical constitution.

Nothing, therefore, can be more desirable than "a healthy soul in a sound body." When we enjoy this divine favor, we can use the healthful powers of our body to enlarge our circle of labor and influence, and by our bright eye, our joyful countenance, and cheerful disposition, we will attract a distrustful world to the service of our blessed Redeemer.

But although physical health is a most desirable blessing to the Christian, in order to recommend the Gospel to others, and to do the work of the Master enthusiastically and efficiently, yet *our spiritual prosperity is not dependent upon this*. We find healthy souls in the feeblest and most sickly bodies.

Many a Christian, whose spirit soars without restraint to its loved home in heaven, must exclaim with the great Paul, "in this tabernacle we groan, being burdened." It is a lamentable fact, that where we observe unbroken physical health, and worldly prosperity, we commonly find a low degree of spiritual life. And it is, alas, but too true, that, inorder to find a thoroughly developed spiritual life and unwavering faith in God, we must go to the huts of poverty or to the gloomy sick-chambers.

A few years ago a poor man died near Boston, whom the newspapers described as having lain thirty years on his back, in a state of helplessness and torment almost incredible.

During the whole period he was unable to raise *a hand.* He could not move himself on his bed, nor masticate his food—a thin liquid, sucked in by his lips, being all that supported nature. Every day he was seized with spasms which convulsed his whole frame so fearfully, that the spectacle could not be endured, and visitors were obliged to leave the room.

Yet, in the midst of all, he was continually praising God for his unspeakable mercy—declaring to those around how happy he was in the opportunity of glorifying the grace of that Savior, who had plucked him, a poor worthless brand, from the burning.

Yes, how often God must rob men of their health, and visit them with the most painful afflictions, in order to secure the prosperity of their souls.

In order to cure the crafty Jacob of his deceitful practice and too great selfconfidence, God had to touch the hollow of his thigh, and to make him cripple for life. In order that the celebrated Paul, who had been caught up in the third Heavens, might be kept from *pride,* a painful thorn in the flesh was sent him, which, in spite of his earnest supplicating prayers, remained.

When Samson in the glory of his strength laid his head in Delilah's lap, and was bound by the chains of lust, he thought not of God; but when his eyes were bored out, and his soul was filled with anguish and despair he turned his ball-less sockets to God, and earnestly besought his pardoning grace. When Nebuchadnezzar dwelt in power and glory in his splendid palace at Babylon, he vaunted in his acquisitions and accomplishments; but when he was afflicted with the worst of all maladies, he lifted his eyes to Heaven, and blessed the Most High, and praised and honored Him, that lives forever. Not unfrequently disease has proved the greatest blessing which God could send to an individual or a family. While physical health, therefore, is very desirable and may enhance our happiness and usefulness as

Christians, yet it is by no means indispensable, and has even proved in many cases a spiritual disadvantage. We should ever remember the answers which Paul received, to his most earnest prayers—"My grace is sufficient for thee, for my strength is made perfect in weakness." Let us glory, therefore, with the apostle in infirmities, that the power of Christ may rest upon us.

An aged woman, who had become deaf and blind, said to one at her side, whose pity she seemed to feel "You're mourning for me, my dear, and there is no need. I am as happy as a child. I sometimes think I am a child, whom the Lord is hush-a-bying to my long sleep. For when I was a nurse girl my missus always telled me to speak very soft and low, to darken the room, that her little one might go to sleep; and now all voices are hushed and still to me, and the bonny earth seems dim and dark, and I know it's my Father lulling me away to my long sleep. I am well content and you need n't feel for me."

No my friends, physical health is not absolutely necessary, inorder to be a happy and useful Christian.

He, who in the midst of earthly calamities and increasing danger, can sing with the prophet "although the fig-tree shall not blossom, neither shall fruit be in the vine; the labor of the olive shall fail and the fields shall yield no meat; the flock shall be cut off from the fold, and there shall be no herd in the stalls; yet, I will rejoice in the Lord, I will joy in the God of my salvation," can also say with the afflicted servant of the Lord, when, after all these calamities and trials, the precious treasure of health is taken away from him, "the Lord gave and the Lord hath taken away, blessed be the name of the Lord."

3. "Beloved, I wish above all things, that thou mayest prosper and be in health, even as thy soul prospereth."

This wish of Jesus' faithful disciple suggests another practical thought, viz: that the *prosperity of our soul is of the very highest importance.*

St. John values physical health very highly. He ranks it above every earthly blessing, but not above the interests of our immortal soul. Alas! that any should do this! Alas, that there should be those, who pray for themselves, and their friends, with this inspired apostle, "above all things, that they may prosper and be in health," but who omit the last clause, who CANNOT, who DARE NOT use this phrase, because their soul does not prosper, but is afflicted with sore complaints.

How many there are, who think about everything except the prosperity of their poor soul. They would continue to forget s interests, did not sickness occasionally come, as a reminder. And even then they would give it no thought, if it were not for the fact, that sickness is a forerunner of death, and that conscience accords with the sentence of God's word—"it is appointed unto men once to die, but after this the judgment."

It is the thought of death and judgment, which in the hour of severe sickness causes some, momentarily at least, to desire and pray for the salvation of their soul. When they observe that the king of terrors is approaching them, and that the world with all its charms is vanishing from their sight, then they begin to call for mercy.

All through life they wish and pray for all other things; but their last wish, which they utter with trembling breath, is: "O God, that my soul may prosper."—Just the reverse is the conduct of the apostle of love. The very first thing to which he looks is that the soul of his friend prospereth and is in health. All other desires are repressed, and subordinate to this. Without a healthy soul, physical health was but little worth in his estimation.

This is everything. He is assured of the healthful spiritual condition of this brother, whom he loves in the truth.

He has seen with his own eyes how he forsook the debasing service of idols, and became a devoted follower of his Master.

He has carefully watched his growth in grace. Recently the brethren, who visited him, brought glad tidings concerning his spiritual state. They told him how God, "who forgiveth all our iniquities, and who healeth all our diseases," had renewed his spiritual youth like the eagle's, and, therefore, he prays, that his physical condition may be as good as his spiritual condition. "Beloved, I wish above all things, that thou mayest prosper and be in health, *even as* thy soul prospereth." Had his spiritual state been otherwise than it was, how differently he would have been addressed by the apostle. Words of exhortation and warning would have flowed from his pen.

Bitter medicine would he have administered to him, in order that his soul might be healed.

But he need not do this, for it is well with his soul. How he has ascertained this cheering fact, he proceeds to tell in the short epistle addressed to him.

"I rejoiced greatly, when the brethren came and testified of the truth that is in thee, even as thou walkest in the truth."

He expresses his intense delight concerning this, when he says "I have no greater joy than to hear that my children walk in the truth." And still further, he shows how the true spiritual prosperity of Gaius manifests itself abroad. "Beloved, thou doest faithfully whatever thou doest to the brethren, and to the strangers—which have borne witness of thy charity before the Church."

Happy disciple, concerning whom such things can be written, whose pastor, when he would wish him temporal prosperity, can do this no better, than by adopting his spiritual prosperity as its measure, and say, "may your body prosper as much as your soul prospers."

Such a one may lack everything else that is valuable. A coarse and patched garment may cover his body; an unsightly cabin may shelter him from the storms of day, and the dangers of night, a bare crust may be his daily fare; yet who, that has learned to estimate spiritual prosperity, will not greet him as a rich and highly favored being?

Would that we might all enjoy that high measure of spiritual health, that Gaius did! How much happier we would be; for truly, my friends, happiness does not consist in the vastness of our possessions, nor in the greatness of our honors, nor in the multitude of our pleasures, but in *what we are.*

The first thing, that we should seek, therefore, is a soul at home with God, purified through the blood of Christ. We should not let this go, as is so common, until sickness arrests us in our earthly toil, or the shadows of life's evening fall upon our path. I

(7)

all of us should ask this morning of God, that He might give us just as much material prosperity, just as much physical health, as our souls prospered, would not the condition of many be sad indeed? Would you venture to offer this prayer for yourself? Would you respond "Amen," if it were offered for you from the pulpit? Would you not tremble, if God should comply with this request?

Gaius will rejoice, if this wish of his spiritual father be fulfilled.

Would you have reason for joy, if you received material and physical prosperity, *even* as your soul prospered? We fear not. No, we would not dare to offer this prayer for each one of you.

We would be your enemy, if we did. Alas, what a sad and visible change would come over this entire congregation, if our temporal and physical prosperity should be gauged by our spiritual prosperity.

No epidemic of the worst kind would create such consternation and panic in this community, and there would probably be few doctors able to prescribe for the sick—and perhaps few Christians to pray for the dying.

The sound of mirth and gladness would be no longer heard in our streets. But a wail more lamentable than that, which was heard throughout Egypt during that eventful night, when the Israelites bade farewell to their house of bondage, would ascend to heaven from our homes and streets.

All business would be stopped. The plough would stand untouched in the furrows, and few hands would be found to glean the autumn fruit. What a terrible calamity, if the prayer of the text were answered, and our bodies brought into essential union with our souls—our physical condition answering to our spiritual condition. If a diseased soul could transmute its maladies, and transfer them into bodily ailments, the whole world would be transformed into a vast lazaretto in which there would be few nurses and millions of patients. For how few of us, my friends, could an apostle offer the prayer—how few of us dare offer it for ourselves—that our "bodily health may be *even* as the health of our souls."

These things, my brethren, ought not so to be! We should prize soul-health above every other blessing. We should not be satisfied for one moment without this highest gift of heaven. It only has intrinsic value.

What a precarious thing bodily health is! To-day we are strong and vigorous. We perform our accustomed labor cheerfully and without distressing fatigue. We run and do not grow weary; we walk and faint not, and it seems as if we have scores of years of life before us. But to-morrow or next day, the blinds of store or work-shop are shut—there is a crape on the door—the owner or proprietor of the establishment, who so recently boasted of health and strength, has suddenly fallen before the king of terrors. What has this poor man now of all for which he has toiled in the sweat of his brow? As we brought nothing into this world, it is certain we can carry nothing out.

His soul is the only possession he carries with him into the unseen world. What if this soul has not prospered, if its cries have been unheeded, if it has suffered hunger and nakedness! "What is a man profiteth, if he shall gain the whole world, and lose his own soul?" There are no interests, which we ought to take more to heart than those, which pertain to our immortal spirit.

We ought not to consent to be more rich or prosperous in worldly, than in spiritual treasures.

Beloved, do you realize, that you have been too neglectful about your highest concerns?

Do you feel like exclaiming " my leanness, my leanness, woe unto me?" We point you to the Great Healer, and say in the language of the prophet—" Is there no balm in Gilead? Is there no physician there, why then is not the health of the daughter of my people recovered."

If the spiritnal disorders of your souls have not been eradicated, if the leprosy of sin, or the cancer of unbelief has not been cured, go to him, who healeth all manner of diseases, and who has said for our encouragement, to those who would bar the way to him, "they that are whole need not the physician, but they that are sick." Go to him, therefore; show him all your wounds and complaints. Remember " that there is life for a look at the crucified one. There is life at this moment for thee. Then look, sinner, look unto him and be saved. Unto him, who was nailed on the tree."

Heart-giving.

My son, give me thine heart.
Prov. 23:26.

PRAYER is a human necessity. It is the result of our total dependence upon a higher power. Hence its practice is not confined to those nations, which have been blessed with the light of revelation, but it co-extends with the race.

We cannot get along without prayer. We are constantly, and often unconsciously asking. We are in need of a thousand things every day of our life. Each hour brings new wants, every emergency its peculiar petition. The Bible from beginning to end is full of encouragement to prayer. Its entire import is "ask and ye shall receive." But in our text we have a most singular suppliant, as well as a most singular request.

It is the great and infinite God, the Creator of the ends of the earth, who stands at the door of his earth-born creature in the humble attitude of a petitioner. He, who ever does exceeding abundantly above what we are able to ask or think, comes to us, and says GIVE ME! What marvelous condescension! Let us listen to this august suppliant, and learn what he so urgently desires.

It is not many things he calls for. His prayer is not an indefinite one. His whole heart is set on one thing, and for this he begs and pleads with more than human eloquence—"My son give me thine heart."

By the term "heart," as here employed, we are, of course, not to understand that bunch of muscles, which beats the blood through that vast network of elastic arteries, which runs through our entire physical organism. Nor is it intended to represent man's emotional nature, or the fountain of his affections and sympathies, in contradistinction from his intellectual powers. It is the *inner man*, or, as the apostle Peter expresses it "the hidden man of the heart."

To give our heart to a person, or object, is to center our strongest affections upon him or it. To do this, it is not necessary, that the object be in our immediate vicinity. Time and distance cannot sever the heart from the object around which its warmest affections are entwined. Locally the object may be as far distant as the antipodes, or as the heavens are from the earth. Still the man is there, though his body may be confined to some small spot on earth. Man is so great, that earth cannot hold him. His thoughts and aspirations outrun the speed of the lightning, yea, the rapidity of the swift-winged angel.

He has this remarkable power, that he can lead two lives; one amid the animal creation here below, and the other above in the society of Christ and redeemed spirits. The Christian, who is risen with Christ in newness of life, sets his affections on things above.

There is his *real* life, because his *heart* is there. When Paul and Silas were cast into the gloomy dungeon at Philippi with their feet in the torturing stock, their hearts were with their glorified Savior in heaven. Cheered by his divine presence and sustaining grace, they became oblivious to the pain of their mangled flesh, and swollen feet, and made the very midnight air vocal with their songs of praise.

We often hear people speak of giving their hearts to God in a very flippant way, as if this was the easiest, and the most natural thing for man to do. While the fact is, that it is the most difficult task to which a rebellious sinner is called. Man is haughty, proud, self-willed. "We will not have this man reign over us," is the voice of the natural heart. He steels and bars his heart against God, as if he were the most defiant robber.

What shameful abuses, what constant insults God must endure before the door is opened, and a gentle voice from within responds: " Come in thou blessed of the Lord, wherefore standest thou without." But in the spirit of the most astonishing patience, this divine suppliant stands waiting and knocking at the heart-door, while the hours are fast rolling by, and his very locks are wet with the dew of night.

His whole mind and heart are set on securing an entrance there. For well he knows, if he gains admission to the heart, he has possession of the whole man.

What the sun is to the solar system the heart of man is to his entire moral being, and all its concomitants.

Everything revolves around that heart. Its laws of attraction are all-controlling and all-governing.

The little infant in the cradle is the monarch of the house, and his wants are attended to with the utmost promptness and precision, because he has the heart of that ministering mother. If God has our heart, all that we have and are is entirely at his disposal. He will then have the power of our intellect, the eloquence of our lips, the skill of our hands, and the swiftness of our feet. The hours of our life will be his, and the gold and silver, that we have acquired, will be laid at his feet. The constant prayer of the soul will be "Lord, what wilt thou have me to do," or "Here am I, send me." What was the great secret of Paul's life, who labored so zealously for his Master, who feared no dangers, who counted no sacrifices, who hazarded his life in planting Churches, and in bringing souls under the power and subjection of the Gospel?

Certainly there could be no selfishness, nor vain-glory in all this; for what things were gain to him he counted loss. The secret motive of that most remarkable of all lives was the constraining force of *Christian love.* Jesus had his heart so completely, that he could not but abound in labors and sufferings for him. In like manner, if he has our hearts entirely and unreservedly, there will be no lack of doing and giving with us.

"Out of the heart," says Solomon, "are the issues of life." And he, who has the fountain, must also have the streams which it sends forth.

Jonathan gave his regal vesture, his bow and sword, yea, his very kingdom, to David, because, as we read again and again, "he loved him as his own soul."

If God has not our hearts, *he has really nothing*. We may intend to be very liberal with him. We may regularly appear within his courts upon his holy day. We may mingle our voice in the worship of song. Our gold or silver may glitter among the offerings of his house. But all this has no value in his sight, if it be not accompanied with the heart. He asks of all our religious performances, of our holiest deeds and of our most reverend acts, how much of the heart is there in them? It is that alone which gives value and fragrance to them. This is the standard by which he measures all our religious services.

The zeal and precision of the most devoted Pharisee, without the heart, is hollow pretension, and the most shocking blasphemy. God asks not yours, but you, and although you understood all mysteries and all knowledge, and although you bestowed your goods to feed the poor, and though you gave your body to be burned for the truth's sake—" verily I say unto you, it would profit you nothing, unless with and above this a voice had spoken within—"I am the Lord's now and forever."

We cannot but notice the difference between the requirements of the true and false religions, that have existed among men. The religions, which are of human devices, are extremely unreasonable in their demands.

They exact much and give us nothing in return. Fanaticism asks for our gold. Mohammedanism demands from its worshippers their sword with which to persecute the followers of the Christ of Calvary. Moloch with his outstretched arms of fire demands of the poor Heathen mother the smiling babe of her bosom. Boudha calls for the life of his devotees and leads them to dream, that self-annihilation is the highest possible felicity.

But the God of revelation, who respects man's moral nature, makes no such demands. He simply asks: "give me thy love." He asks for *nothing more*; but will be satisfied with nothing less. If you could gather all the silver and gold, which the mines of earth contain, and lay it at his feet, it would be an offering far too mean.

Yea, if all Carmel were turned into an immense altar, and all the trees of Lebanon were piled upon its majestic top for a burning, and the cattle upon a thousand hills were sacrificed for a burnt-offering, so that the cloud of its incense would roll heavenward and conceal the very splendors of the noonday sun, what value would all this have!

Is not the earth the Lord's and the fulness thereof? In all this vast Universe there is only one thing, which is not his, my friends; it is your *heart*—and for that he earnestly pleads.

But why does he ask for it?

1. First of all BECAUSE YOU ARE COMPELLED TO DISPOSE OF IT. You are compelled to do so, not by any outward coercion, but by an inward pressure, by the cravings of your own nature. It is as necessary for the soul to love, as it is for the body to breathe.

The hunger of the heart to love is the strongest of all the deep necessities of our nature. As a man with a ravenous appetite will eat with relish the most loathsome food, so the heart, voracious to love, will sometimes settle down upon some mean, contemptible object, rather than not love at all. A prisoner, who was for a long time immured in a gloomy dungeon, and deprived of all human society, in the deep necessity of his nature tamed a spider upon which he lavished his affection, until his cruel jailer brutally destroyed it.

It is of the very highest importance, therefore, that we select the noblest and grandest object upon which to centre our love, because the heart is gradually transformed into the object of its love. In all the Universe we cannot find a more worthy personage, than the Lord Jesus Christ. No matter how low or degraded a person may have become, he may almost have descended below the level of the brutes, yet, through intercourse with him, he may be lifted up to the very fellowship and service of angels. If the eye of the soul catches the brightness of the incarnate God, and fastens its affections upon him, a divine metamorphosis will take place in that soul, and it will gradually be transformed into the same image from glory to glory.

2. Again, God asks for our hearts, because *he would do no violence to our moral nature by wresting it from us.* If man had

no power over his affections, he would be at the mercy of circumstances. He would not be a free man, but a slave. He would be an engine driven by force, and not a free agent responsible to moral law. God, therefore, instead of capturing the citadel of the heart by force, besieges and storms it with the battering rams of love, and seeks to move the sinner to a cheerful surrender of himself. Our salvation, therefore, depends upon our personal choice. Even the Almighty will not save us, except we let him. There is, in one sense, a limit even to his omnipotence; it will never ignore the human will. What a tremendous responsibility, therefore, is human volition! This exalts us far above the material universe. Grand and magestic is the shoreless ocean, whose hidden depths no mortal can explore —and we are filled with awe and holy wonder, as we see its mighty dashing billows leap like mountains to the skies.

As we stand upon its wave-beaten shore with a heart filled with anxiety for the thousands, that are drifting upon its angry bosom, and the corpse of some brave sailor lad, the only son of a widowed mother, is cast at our feet, we say, "the ocean is cruel."

But the ocean is utterly unconscious of the mischief it has done. Yon alps, whose sublime peaks are lost in the clouds, and whose fatal avalanches bury whole villages, which cluster in their sequestered nooks, into utter ruin, are not conscious of their own grandeur and destructive power. They are but obeying the laws of their existence.

But man far transcends these grand works of the Almighty's hands. He is not only a possessor of consciousness, which matter does not possess, but he also enjoys intelligence. Look up to the dazzling skies above our heads. What wisdom and power are here displayed. But man is far greater even than the sun with all his faithful escort of stars. Go with me to some remote and dismal garret, and there, upon a handful of straw, lies a poor, pale, hardlived man, who is greater than these glittering orbs.

It is true, one stroke of that sun or one flash of lightning would destroy him, and yet he can make that sun his vassal and the lightning his messenger. But greater power than all this has man in the superb gift of freedom. He can choose good or evil, life or death. The consequences of the mighty power of individual volition last throughout unnumbered ages. God, in his infinite plan of salvation, takes cognizance of human volition, and treats us like moral creatures. He comes to us and says: "Give me thine heart." He will reason with you, he will entreat you, he will implore you, he will adjure you, but he will never, *never force* you. The choice is wholly yours. Who does not, when he thinks of it, stand abashed at the awful majesty of man?

But let us us look at *some reasons*, why your heart should be given to God.

First of all. Because *no one has such a claim upon it*. It is his own. He made it for himself. He impressed his own image upon it. He endowed it with its fathomless susceptibilities and amazing powers.

To withhold it from him, is the worst of robbery. But God does not only sustain to us the relation of Creator, he is our FATHER. No, it is not a stranger, who is so tenderly pleading for your heart; but it is your Heavenly Father, who speaks—*"my son, give me thine heart."*

You stand in no such intimate relation to any creature as you stand to God. No such claim has a father upon the love and obedience of his son. No such claim has the mother upon the smile of her infant; no such claim has the bride upon the hand and the heart of the bridegroom; no such claim has the brave philanthropist on the grateful recognition of him, whose life he saved, as God has upon our deepest and warmest love. With what mercies he crowns our days. He makes our earthly cup to run over with blessings. It is he, that gives us our physical health, our cheerful firesides, and all the ministries of kindness. Sooner might we undertake to number the stars, than reckon up the multitude of his gifts. But the crown and glory of all God's benefactions is the unspeakable gift of his only-begotten Son. When we think of its amazing excellence and the infinite price of this sacrifice, human language is inadequate to set forth God's claims upon our immortal being. In view of Calvary we may well say to God, now I know, that thou lovest man, seeing that thou hast not withheld thy son, thine only son, from him."

2. Another reason, why we should give our hearts to God is, *because he alone can satisfy it.* Agur speaks of three things, that are never satisfied, yea four, which never say, "it is enough." He might easily have added, a fifth, viz: "the human heart." "You might as soon"—says a quaint old writer—" fill a bag with wisdom and a chest with virtue, or a circle with a triangle, as the heart of man without God."

A man may have enough of the world to sink in, but he can never have enough to satisfy him. You may as well attempt to fill two chasms with each other, as to fill the human heart with earthly good. Sooner can the body be nourished by whirlwinds and dust, than the spirit with things of mere time and sense. But God answers the deepest needs of the aching heart.

In possession of him, the heart exclaims—" Whom have I in Heaven but thee, and there is none upon earth that I desire besides thee. My flesh and my hearth faileth, but God is the strength of my heart and my portion for ever." He is the satisfaction of the heart even in the most distressing circumstances; when all human comforts fail, the rock of our salvation remains firm and unshaken. As the veins in the earth are made for the precious metal, as the rich pasture is created for the grazing flock, and as they in their turn are created for man, so man is made for God. A poor ignorant slave, talking of heaven, when asked by Prof. Stowe, "how she knew that there was any such place," replied, "why, because I have got such a *hankering* for it." The wisest philosopher could not have presented a better argument. But what is Heaven without God? A celebrated infidel writer, in spite of himself, has written these striking words, that if God did not exist, man would have to invent him, in order that he might not sink away into despair. God in Christ satisfies all the needs of the human soul for time and for eternity.

When all things else pass away, he remains its immovable prop and stay.

A father was dying, and as his friends were gathered around his bedside to witness his departure, they anxiously desired one expression of recognition, but his faculties seemed faded, and his memory a blank. One by one they approached him with the question—"Father do you remember me?" but there was no reply. And then all making way for his venerable companion, who had journeyed so many years with him, and shared life's bitter and sweet, his wife drew near. She bends over him, and as the tears fell thick and fast upon his sunken cheeks, she cries "do you not remember me?" A vacant stare was all the reply to that loving question. There was no soul in that filmy eye, and the seal of death was upon these lips. Finally one present, remembering, that the love of Christ was stronger than death which many waters cannot quench, stooped to his dull ear, and said "Do you remember Jesus Christ? No sooner were the words uttered, than the spirit seemed to return, hovering for a moment, ere it took its wings to Heaven. And with a smile in which the soul passed away to glory, he exclaimed: "Remember Jesus Christ, dear Jesus Christ, he is all my salvation, and all my desire."

3. Once more. God should have our heart *because he alone can develop it*.

The human soul is so constituted, that without love to God there is no possibility of having all its powers quickened and developed. What the sun-beam is to the earth, the love of God is to the soul. What glory and fruitfulness is developed beneath the quickening rays of the summer's sun. In like manner the most astonishing excellences are called forth in our lives and character by the indwelling power of God.

The human mind can form no adequate conception of the possibilities, which slumber in the soul. All depends upon the object which shall win the heart. If we surrender it to the world, it will become depraved and sensual, and sink to the deepest depths of hell. If we give it to God, it willl share in the fullest and highest development, and will be transformed into his own blessed image.

"Beloved, now we are the sons of God, but it doth not yet appear what we shall be. But we know that when he shall appear, we shall be like him, for we shall see him as he is."

In view of these facts, we ought to take pleasure in giving to God the offering he desires. But alas! how many shrink back from this divine entreaty, as if it were the most painful task to which men could be called.

It is not once or twice merely, that God is obliged to present his request, but as he came to Samuel at different watches of the night, so he comes to us at different periods of our lives, and it often takes a long time before the sinner discerns his voice and says—"speak Lord, thy servant heareth."

Verily, if his patience was not wonderful, even as his love is amazing, he would long since have said, "let him alone, Ephraim is joined to his idols." The great difficulty is, that the human heart has so many suitors. There is as much strife about it, as there was about the body of Moses. Give me thine heart, say riches. Give me thine heart, says pleasure. Give me thine heart, says fame. Give me thine heart, says ambition. Each claimant urges his peculiar advantages, and, with the tempter of old, places us on some summit from which he discloses to our eager eyes all the splendours and glories of earth, which will be ours, if we will but fall down and worship him. Few learn betimes to see his cunning and sophisty, and to say with our victorious Lord—"Get thee hence Satan; for it is written, thou shalt worship the Lord thy God, and him only shalt thou serve." Yes, the great difficulty is, that your heart is no longer yours. You have already given it to some other object, and to tear it away from it seems like the cutting off of a hand, and the pulling out of an eye. You would be willing, perhaps, to divide the throne of your heart with God, but you will not give him absolute supremacy, and he will not have your heart on any other condition. He that loveth father or mother more than him is not worthy of him. He that loveth son or daughter more than him is not worthy of him. Alas, how great is the folly of multitudes, who, for a momentary pleasure, will imperil the eternal salvation of their souls.

Lysimachus, when he was besieged by the Goths, felt the agonies of a raging thirst, and offered his kingdom to his foes, for a refreshing draught of water. When his thirst was slaked he exclaimed in heart-broken anguish—" O, wretched man that I am, who for so little enjoyment have given so great a kingdom." This will be the cry, that shall re-echo through the caverns of the lost, and very often, even on this side of the grave, men begin to realize the supreme folly of bartering their soul for a moment's pleasure. We beseech you, therefore, most earnestly, give your heart to God. Then happiness will be yours now and forever. Let this matter be quickly decided, for it is of supreme importance.

When the celebrated Sir Raleigh closed his illustrious career on the scaffold of his ungrateful country, he was asked by the executioner, as his head was laid upon the block, whether it lay right, and his heroic answer was—"It matters little, my friend, how the *head* lies, provided the *heart* is right." The day is soon coming when our heads shall toss and turn on death's uneasy pillow, and we shall feel the power of this assertion. Let our hearts therefore be stayed on God, and his eternal arm shall be beneath our head, and we shall sink in sweet repose.

> Ever let thy grace surround me,
> Strengthen me with power divine;
> Till thy cords of love have bound me,
> Make me to be wholly thine.

Lost Penny.

> Either what woman having ten pieces of silver, if she lose one piece, doth not light a candle and sweep the house and seek diligently till she find it? And when she hath found it, she calleth her friends and neighbors together, saying, rejoice with me, for I have found the piece which I had lost. Likewise, I say unto you, there is joy in the presence of the angels of God over one sinner that repenteth.
> Luke 15:8-10.

THE great beauty of our Savior's teaching is, that he does not deal with truth in the abstract, but in the concrete.

His illustrations, which are largely taken from every day life, are full of force and strikingly real. We are made spectators of the incidents he narrates. We can almost see them transpire before our eyes.

This, too, is the case with this simple domestic occurrence so vividly sketched in the text.

At first glance, this parable seems to be identical with that of the lost sheep, which has just preceded it. But upon a closer inspection we learn, that it is no mere repetition of the truth already expressed. It throws new light upon the subject of man's lost condition and God's efforts and interest in his salvation.

These three parables in the fifteenth chapter of Luke constitute a three-fold cord, which is not easily broken. They are as eparably one. They are three windows looking out in different directions, through which we can see the amazing depth of our misery and the unfathomable love of God. Each one must deepen the blush of shame upon the cheeks of those haughty Pharisees, who had so scornfully said of Jesus, "this man receiveth sinners and eateth with them," as this Master Artist illustrates, with increasing force and matchless pathos, the raptures of heaven over the recovery of the lost.

In this parable, as in that of the lost sheep, we have, under altogether different imagery, vividly depicted

I. A GREAT LOSS.
II. A DILIGENT SEARCH.
III. A JOYFUL RECOVERY.

The loss sustained by the woman does not seem to be as great as that sustained by the shepherd. What comparison of value is there between a sheep and a coin. But this only betrays our ignorance of oriental life. Those well acquainted with the domestic habits of the people of Palestine inform us, that even to this day, the jewels of a Syrian woman consist largely of pieces of money. "They are her exclusive property, which her husband may not claim, and, having descended to her as heirlooms from her mother, they are handed down by her to her daughters. They are commonly worn tied in the hair, and the larger pieces generally hanging from the ends of the braids.

Thus one falling out of the hair might be readily lost; while as it formed a part of the dowry of the woman, in which all her descendants had an interest, as well as she, we can easily see, how its loss and recovery would be equally affecting to them all.

Then, if we bear in mind the proportion of that, which was lost to that which still remained, which here was one to ten, and in the other case was one to a hundred, we notice in these parables a climactic order.

The figure, under which the lost sinner is represented here, is quite striking. He is compared to a coin. Not to a mere piece of precious metal, but to a well rounded and stamped coin, upon which the king's image and superscription were impressed, and which bore witness to his authority in the wide range of its circulation. You will remember how on one occasion our Lord's

(8)

ever vigilant enemies sought to entangle him, and approached him with the question, whether it was lawful to give tribute to Cæsar or not. He requested, that they should bring him a coin; and when it was placed in his hands, he asked, "whose is this image and superscription?" And when they replied Cæsar's, he said, "render, therefore, unto Cæsar the things, which are Cæsar's, and to God the things, which are God's."

From this reply of the Savior, we learn that a coin is not only designed as a medium of exchange, but gives testimony to the royalty and right of him, whose image it bears.

Now this is the two-fold purpose of our creation.

We are of no mean origin. We are children of the King of Heaven. God is our Father in the highest and truest sense.

He enstamped his own image upon us. He made us like to himself in the powers of the mind, and in the dignity of our souls. No coin ever issued from the mint so beautiful and glittering, as man came from the hands of his Maker.

In his creation the heavenly intelligences rejoiced, and God was glorified. He bore cheerful testimony to the rightfulness of his Creator's authority, and the ligitimacy of his throne.

But alas! this can no longer be said. "How is the gold become dim! how is the most fine gold changed."

Man is a lost coin, tarnished and corroded by sin, and buried beneath the foulness and the dust of corruption.

The image of his lawful Sovereign has disappeared, and he no longer serves the grand purpose of his existence. God is not glorified in him. He no longer reflects his image. He no longer proclaims his Sovereignty.

The coin might just as well have been non existent, as far as the benefit of the owner was concerned. As long as it was lost, it was of no use to any one. The same is true with regard to fallen man.

He confers no glory upon God, he bears no witness to his power and excellency. On the contrary, he positively dishonors him, and in those parts of his nature, in which he resembles him most nearly, he is most emphatically lost. His reason has become blinded by sin and no longer entertains the knowledge of

God. His affections have been alienated from him and are centred upon earthly objects. His will is perverse and prone to evil. His life is debased and godless. Other gods reign over him, and he is a willing captive of the god of this world, who has blinded his mind, and holds him in thraldom. He is lost. But though lost, he is not *worthless*. The coin, if recovered, would still be as valuable as ever. Although it is blackened with rust and covered with dust, it is still precious silver, and here and there a letter of its original superscription may be deciphered, and a faint trace of its noble Sovereign be discerned. Man, no matter how low he may sink in the scale of being, shows distinct traces of his exalted origin.

We speak of bestial men, but there is no comparison between the highest brute and the highest type of a reasonable man. There is a wide, yawning, impassable gulf between the human and the brute creation, which no evolutionist can span. Even in the very heart of heathendom, where the light of Gospel truth and civilization have not penetrated, we discern the nobility of man in his towering reason, soaring ambition, deep aspiration for immortality.

No matter how he may be polluted by sin, we may here and there distinctly discern the sparkling of the silver and gold of his original existence.

Man, though lost, is not *hopelessly lost*. The coin is lost in the house. Had the woman lost it while crossing the wild and trackless moor, or had she dropped it in the unfathomed depths of Ocean, it would have been gone forever.

But since it has dropped from her while engaged in the house, it may be found again, even though it had rolled into the darkest corner. No sinner, therefore, is beyond the reach of recovery. Though vile and polluted, he may be washed and arrayed in the clean linen of Christ's righteousness. The original likeness of his God may be reproduced in him.

There are things which can never be renewed. The beautiful white snow, that we tread beneath our feet and mingles with the mud of our streets, no alchemist can bleach into its original purity.

A handsome mirror, that is smashed into a hundred pieces,

can never be restored to its place upon the parlor wall. What act can restore the freshness and fragrance of the faded flower? But man, though deeply fallen, can be brought back to his pristine glory. Infinite possibilities lie wrapped up in his soul.

The throne of heaven is encircled with happy beings robed in snowy vestments, who once were vile and impure.

What an incentive, then, do we have here to labor in behalf of the lost, to bring the missing coin back to heaven's treasury.

This leads us to speak of

II. The Diligent Search, spoken of in our parable.

Before we proceed with the interpretation of this matchless parable, we should have a clear and definite conception of the oriental home in which the coin was lost.

This will aid us in the understanding of the imagery employed. The houses in the East were constructed differently than ours are.

Owing to the intensity of the heat, they had but few windows, and even these were covered all over with lattice work, so that the sunlight, which is so welcome with us, was excluded, and the house wrapped in darkness.

If, therefore, anything was lost, it required, even in broad day light, the light of a candle to find it.

Nor was there visible in the oriental house that cleanliness, which usually accompanies godliness. The house was commonly confused and in an untidy condition.

As the floors were formed of dried mud, and covered with rushes, which were renewed only at rare intervals, a vast amount of dust and filth would naturally accumulate, in which a piece of money might be easily lost.

This accounts for the lighting of a candle and the sweeping of the house, which was required, in order to bring back the strayed coin from its dusty retreat.

But who is meant by the *woman?* Some Scripture expositors seem to think, that because Christ is represented in the former parable under the beautiful figure of a shepherd, that this same person of the Godhead must be represented under the figure of the lost coin.

But this does not at all follow.

All must be agreed, that God the Father, and not God the Son, is represented to us in the third parable. If this is so, why may not a different person of the holy trinity be represented in the parable before us.

We believe, that in the first parable, we have God the Son represented under the image of the shepherd; in the third, God the Father; and in the second God the Spirit.

We see, then, how the whole Godhead is interested in human salvation. Would you know what Christ has done for us? See how the shepherd left the ninety and nine and subjected himself to the exposure and weariness of the wilderness to find the wandering sheep. Would you know the readiness with which God the Father receives the penitent sinner? Turn to the last parable of this precious chapter. Would you know what part the Holy Spirit takes in working out our redemption? Carefully study this parable before us.

The woman in her work of searching employed two agencies—broom and candle.

The great instrument in the hands of the Holy Spirit for bringing sinners to the light is the lamp of truth.

Without it there can be no conversion. All searching without this illuminating candle is futile. Nor is it truth indiscriminately used, that tends to the saving of the soul, but that truth, which has Christ for its object, who is the real soul of the Gospel—the good news of a purchased salvation—the old theme of "Christ and him crucified," which Paul preached in the heathen cities where he carried the Gospel, and by means of which the face of the world was changed. On the eve of Christ's passion he said to his disciples: "And I, when I be lifted up, will draw all men unto me." The cross of Calvary has been the great attractive centre. They tell us, that in some large millinery establishments, where many needles are lost in the course of a day, instead of going down upon the floor and picking wearily each one up, a young woman goes round at night, holding a magnet near the floor attracting thereby every minutest particle of steel, and so they are all gathered. The great instrument which the

Holy Spirit employs to draw men away from sin to righteousness and holiness, is the magnet of the cross. But not always does this powerfully operate upon the guilty heart. As the magnet will not draw, where there are neutralizing elements near, so the truth fails to perform its mission, when we are attracted by the subtle influences of of perishing world. How many souls there are everywhere, which feel not the drawing power of the Gospel, because they are steeped in sin, engrossed in earthly pursuits or enamored with the fleeting pleasures of time.

Something else, therefore, must be used to destroy these counter attractions of the world.

Or, to return to the figure of the text, the light alone .in the hands of the woman is not sufficient. This might do, if the coin had not dropped on rush-covered floor, and was not buried beneath the dust and debris of an oriental home. In order that the light may fall upon it, everything must be turned upside down. All this has its spiritual significance. The word of God, preached by the most devoted minister of the Gospel, would never turn the heart to the Lord. There are hindrances which must first be removed.

There are preparations which must first be made.

As the fallow ground must be ploughed and harrowed, before the seed can take root, and yield a harvest of golden grain, so in many cases the heart must be made soft and pliant by the plough-share of affliction and the sharp teeth of the harrow of earthly trouble.

Then the seed will germinate and a harvest of spiritual good will ripen. Sweeping must precede or accompany the most brilliantly shining lamp. God sends providential disturbances, losses in business, personal sickness, family bereavement, or the dormant conscience is aroused by an accident, a sudden death or an earnest soul-searching discourse. As the action of the broom produces a cloud of dust, and brings things to light, which have been previously obscured, so these perturbations of the heart reveal its foulness and are preludes to the purity and peace, that follow. As the house cannot be cleansed, and, what is lost within its precincts, cannot be recovered without these trying disturbances, so sinners—especially those, who have been long and deeply sunk in sin, are seldom converted without great trials, agitations and searchings of heart.

If the jailer had not felt the shock of the earthquake, and seen the open doors, and the peril in which he was, he would never have cast himself at the feet of Paul and Silas, crying out "what must I do to be saved!" Let us not murmur, then, when we are disturbed out of our peaceful dreams, but realize, that God by his Holy Spirit is only endeavoring to reclaim what is lost.

Let him not seek us in vain, but let us yield ourselves to him with an undivided heart, saying—"Here Lord, I give myself to thee. 'Tis all that I can do."

When this is done we are the occasion of

III. Unbounded Joy.

The woman, when the light of her candle flashed upon the lost treasure, was filled with joy. This seems no wonder, when we remember that this was a long-treasured heirloom, which had adorned the person of not a few of her ancestral line.

It is true, if she had not regained it, she was still owner of nine pieces. But each one, perhaps, had a unique value.

It is quite probable, that our world is the only one, that has swung "out of its orbit, and has wandered into darkness and away from God," and it is doubtless no fanciful conjecture, that this planet bears no more proportion to the myriad worlds, that roll through space, than does " one quivering leaf to the foliage of the giant trees—it may be—to all the leaves of a boundless forest."

But that makes it none-the-less precious to God.

No, he values each individual soul, as if it were the only one in creation, and breaks out in these melting tones at the sight of its rebellion and waywardness—"How shall I give thee up Ephraim, how shall I deliver thee Israel, how shall I make thee as Admah, how shall I set thee as Zeboim; mine heart is turned within me, my repentings are kindled together."

The woman in the parable could not contain her joy within herself. She summoned her neighbors and friends, saying " Rejoice with me." Joy is naturally diffusive. It ceases to be joy, when it is pent up. We know from our own experience, when we have made some happy discovery, how anxious we are to find some heart with which to share our gladness. People have been known to walk miles and miles to find some one to whom they could communicate their joy. We can imagine how this joy-burdened woman rushed out of the house, and with sparkling eyes told her female friends, who had recently heard of her loss, that the much-prized treasure had been recovered. "Likewise" —says our Savior—" there is joy in the presence of the angels of God over one sinner that repenteth."

It seems, that in this respect also we bear God's image.

He, if we may be allowed to represent Him thus, seems to need or rather, to desire society to make his joy complete. The Lord Jesus Christ, on the very eve of his passion, saw through the rifts of the dark clouds, that veiled his sky, the dazzling splendors of his victory, and could not refrain from the prayer "Father I will, that they also, whom thou hast given me, be with me where I am, that they may behold my glory."

Jesus took three of his disciples with him into the garden of his anguish. He desired fellowship in his suffering.

But sooner might he have suffered alone, than to have enjoyed his glory alone.

We cannot tell with certainty, who these beings are, who are symbolized in the parable by the friends and neighbors.

They must either be unfallen angels or pure beings, who inhabit other worlds, upon whom the blight of sin has never rested, and who are informed of God's deep interest in this little planet of ours.

These noble, sinless beings, who are in perfect accord with God, enter into the spirit of his feelings and break forth into rapturous delight and " strike their harps, and swell their hallelujahs, when through the gates of pearl the ministering angels enter, and announce another sinner saved; another victory for the Redeemer —another trophy of the cross—another brand, plucked from the burning; another gem for the kingly crown of the world's Christ."

From the parable, which we have endeavored to elucidate, it is evident, that the recovery of the vilest and most abandoned sinner is not impossible. Let no sinner despair. Let no one say "my sins are too great or too many."

Neither let us despair of others, for whose conversion we are earnestly praying and anxiously laboring. There is no one beyond the reach of God's omnipotent arm. There is no pollution so great, which the blood of the Lord Jesus Christ cannot remove. His blood eradicates scarlet sins, and makes the foulest whiter than snow.

Despondent sinner, take courage, and remember the beautiful hymn of Charles Wesley

> "Ready for you the angels wait
> To triumph in your blest estate;
> Turning their harps, they long to praise
> The wonders of redeeming grace."

We should also learn from this parable, that as long as we are not earnestly seeking the lost, we may bear the name of a Christian, but are not in sympathy with God and his angelic hosts.

From this beautiful trinity of parables, we learn how every person in the Godhead is taking an active interest in human redemption.

It is God's grandest work. Shall we not then be anxious to be co-laborers with him—sharers of the highest joy, which even deity can know?

Alas, how many a valuable coin is lost in the house, which waits for your efforts to bring it back to its heavenly owner.

Leave no work undone. Avoid no sacrifice. Submit to the humblest task. Be willing to toil among the lowest and vilest, if you can only win them for the Savior.

> Go, brethren on your missions, seek
> The tempted, lost and vile and tried;
> Go to the lowest slums of vice,
> And preach the love of him, who died.
> Go, search the thoroughfares of sins
> With tract and hymn and Gospel truth;
> Go, filled with love, and zeal and fire
> And snatch, from death, our erring youth.
> Go to the sick and dying bed,
> And gently speak of hope in store
> For those, who gaze upon the cross
> Of Him, who lives to die no more.
> This be our mission under God;
> O, may we ever loud proclaim
> The height, and depth and length and breadth,
> Of grace and love in Jesus' name.

No More Sea.

And there shall be no more sea.
Rev. 21:16.

OUR text carries us back to the lonely isle of Patmos, a sterile rock in the Ægean Sea, about eighteen miles in circumference, where John, the bosom friend of our Savior, was banished for the word of God and the testimony of Jesus Christ.

It was, no doubt, a sad hour to this Patriarch of the Apostles when he was obliged to quit his field of Christian toil and delightful associations at Ephesus, and was driven to these inhospitable shores. But God could have conferred no such honor upon him amid his kindred and friends in the Asiatic Metropolis as he did in these dreary solitudes. Patmos has forever immortalized his name. Like another Moses, our Lord closeted this faithful Boanerges with him in the Mount, and showed him the Pattern of the real tabernacle, which God built and not man. Upon the first day of the week, when he was far away from God's earthly courts, and his soul was lost in Heavenly musings, the Lord of glory himself appeared amid the bleak rocks of his solitary home, and turned rough Patmos into a veritable Bethel. No mortal ever received such celestial visitation, and caught such bright glimpses of the glories of a world to come. Many a book has been written, the loss of which the World would never have felt.—But this cannot be said of the book, which closes the N. T. canon.

What comforting promises, what solemn warnings, what glorious visions, we would have missed, if divine providence had not led the Apostle to this place of retirement. Then the immortal works of Bunyan and Milton would never have seen the light. The lover of Christian truth and sublime literature never tires of perusing these closing chapters of the Bible. What magnificent descriptions of our future home! All the wealth and grandeur of the Universe is summoned to aid us in our conceptions of its exalted nature. The uninspired mind has never conceived of anything half so grand, as the new Jerusalem which breaks upon the gaze of the rapt seer. Our text gives us one pencil stroke of this exquisite word-painting. "And there shall be no more sea."

Why no more sea?" Can there be anything gratifying in this thought to the beloved disciple, whose past life has been so intimately associated with the deep? Has he not been a constant voyager on its ruffled surface? Has it not in a measure been the the home of this fisherman's son? Can he not sing with the poet

"From a boy."

I wantoned with the breakers—they to me
Were a delight—; and if the refreshing sea
Made them a terror—'t was a pleasing fear,
For I was, as it were, a child of thee,
And trusted to thy billows far and near,
And laid my hand upon thy mane."

I wantoned with the breakers—they to me were a delight.

It was upon its bosom, that for many years he found an honest pursuit, until the Master called him to be a fisher of men. It was upon its bosom, that the Lord once and again surprised him with the most marvellous exhibitions of his divine power and glory. How can he ever forget the sea and those pleasing recollections, that cluster around it!—But the grand majestic oceam is an object of attraction to us all.

Who does not admire the ever changing glory, that it wears in storm and sunshine, and who does not love to listen to its gentle murmurs or the thunders of its roar? The grandest inspirations of human thought have been born of communings with the sea. Well has it been said "A World without the sea would be a World without life, beauty or attraction, a silent realm of desolation and death."

"Summer Ocean; how I'll miss thee,
　Miss the wonders of thy shore;
　Miss the magic of thy grandeur,
　　When the sea shall be no more."

But notwithstanding all this, a little reflection will convince us that Heaven brightens, as we think of it as a place where there will be no more sea, because that means there will be no more *separations.*—That rolling sea, what a mighty barrier it was to this lonely captive of Patmos, whose heart was on the other side. O how often, as he stood upon its shore, did he cast a wishful glance across this waste of waters, which separated him from his brethren and friends at Ephesus.

How dreary and monotonous life must have seemed to him, as he toiled among the mines of this rugged isle, or wrote in the traditional grotto, or wandered companionless along its rockbound coast, listening to the music of the ever restless waves.

"No more sea," could there be a more cheering thought to him? Would it not kindle his desires for Heaven into a still brighter flame? Our lot may not have been cast like that of the beloved disciple on some lonely isle, yet we all know by personal experience the principal meaning of that word "farewell." The mother knows it, who amid choked utterances gives her parting counsel to her boy before he sets out for college life. The son knows it, who is obliged to leave home and his early associations to find employment among strangers. O the tears and headache, as he listens for the last time to his father's prayer in which he is so earnestly commended to God and the word of his grace. The scene upon the shores of Miletus, which is so graphically portrayed by Luke's master-pen, where Paul kneels down in prayer, and the Ephesian Elders fall weeping round his neck and kiss him, has been witnessed more than once. Whose eyes have not at times filled with tears—whose bosom has not heaved with sobs, as the parting word was spoken. How often friends have lingered on the shore, and gazed with wishful eyes after the vessel, that bore away some precious friend, until it was lost to sight on the far horizon. O the feelings of the lonely voyager, as his loved native land fades out of sight, and he realizes, that the separation between him and his friends becomes greater every moment. But it is not always a *watery sea*, that separates us from friends. Between how many hearts, linked together by the warmest ties of affection, rolls the *mystic stream of death*.

Death enters the happiest homes, and plucks off the sweetest flowers.

" Friend after friend departs;
Who has not lost a friend."

What marked changes take place in every family in the course of a single decade. To-day parents and children gather around the evening fireside, and they can hardly realize that this will not last forever; that the first family break must come.—That soon, God knows how soon, the whole family will be scattered and gone, like the brood of young birds in the orchard tree, which yesterday seemed wingless and helpless, and to-day have flown away, and only left an empty nest behind. From how many, that are dear to us, does the Ocean of Time separate us.

How many, that we once knew and loved, have disappeared like billows on the stream of time. What separations have taken place since the hour that the apostle looked up to Heaven, and saw his Lord disappear in a chariot of clouds. Peter has been crucified; Paul's head has fallen by the bloody axe; and James, his brother after the flesh, as well as after the spirit, has received his Master's baptism, and drank of his cup. Of the entire Apostolic College, he is the only survivor. Who knows, but at this very time, he thinks of the language of Christ concerning him "If I will, that he tarry till I come, what is that to thee." O how often, before we ourselves embark to that mystic shore from which none ever returns, are we called upon to wave a tearful adieu to departing friends. In Heaven these sad scenes will never occur. There will be no parting there. There the farewell word will never be spoken. There will be no barriers of distance, language and estrangement among all the countless inhabitants of that vast realm.

Again. There will be no more sea in the future life, because there will be no more *agitation* and *turmoil*. The sea is the emblem of instability. It is in constant commotion. It has its diurnal changes in the ebb and flow of its tides. It is the sport of winds, and is governed by the mysterious influences of the Heavenly bodies.

It is subject to constant fluctuations. Now its surface appears smooth and placid, and in its waters we see the bright moon, and flitting clouds most beautifully mirrored. But the very next hour, it is swept by tempestuous gales, and the fury of its dashing billows strikes the mind with awe and terror.

What a true picture this is of human life in all its vicissitudes. It is a rare instance to meet one whose life moves along in an even tenor from one year to another. The unexpected happens to us all. Man is born unto trouble, as the sparks fly upward.

Each life has its ups and downs. There are no eyes, which have not been fountains of tears. There are no backs, which have not stooped beneath some heavy load. One messenger of sorrow follows quickly upon the heels of another. How many are constrained to say, "when I looked for good, then evil came unto me; and when I waited for light, there came darkness." The spider's most attenuated thread is cord, is cable, to man's feeble tie on earthly bliss.

The Patriarch of Luz, who to-day lives in honor and wealth, and who was a philanthropist of the very highest order, who was eyes to the blind, feet to the lame, a father to the poor, and an heroic defender to the oppressed, sits to-morrow like a vile outcast, broken-hearted, upon a solitary ash-heap.

The cheerful Naomi, whose graceful form, and light step every one knows, as she passes through the streets of Bethlehem, and whose happy lot so many envied, returns after a few years of sojourn abroad, as an indigent, childless, and brokenhearted widow, and every one of her old acquaintances breaks out in perfect astonishment as she passes by her door: "Is this Naomi?" The singularly beautiful garment, with which Jacob robed his favorite child, he presently holds in his hands, all stained with blood, exclaiming "an evil beast hath devoured him, Joseph is without doubt rent to pieces."

In one form or another trouble comes to every human heart. To-day it comes in the form of sickness, tomorrow in the death of friends. Now in the shape of financial loss, then again in the unkind stab on our reputation. It seems that the older we grow, the rougher life's sea becomes, and the more frequent its storms are. No moral excellence or wise precaution can prevent these sweeping gales.

But the end of all these things draws nigh. On the shores of Heaven these storms cease to blow. There will be nothing of this earthly instability. There will be no heaving breasts, no tear-dimmed eyes, no fluttering hearts. There will be no more persecution, no more martyrdom, but eternal rest. Our happiness there will be perfect and undisturbed.—Yes! there will be sea, but it will be a sea of glass mingled with fire. It will not be an unstable or treacherous element, but solid like crystal glass, upon which the Redeemed will stand like mighty conquerors, with the harps of God in their hands and the song of Moses and the Lamb upon their lips.

Again, there "will be no more sea" means, there will be no *more disaster*.

The perils of the sea are proverbial. Who can look upon the vast billowy deep without recalling its searching tales of woe and shipwreck. "They have heard evil tidings; there is sorrow on the sea, it cannot be quiet." Thus does Jeremiah repeat the story of Damascus. Wonderful have been the improvements made during the last few years in the construction of our steamers. They float like immense palaces on the blue deep and bid defiance to the maddest storm. Remarkable also has been the increase of knowledge in the art of navigation and nautical computation. Fog and darkness may shut out the sun by day and the stars at night, yet the captain knows precisely where he is, and can almost to a minute tell when land will be in view. Yet, notwithstanding all these improvements, shipwrecks are of constant occurrence. It is said, that in the gales of a single November a thousand sailors perished on the shores of Great Britain alone.

Hundreds of vessels enter the world's seaports every fall in a dismantled condition. Many leave port and are never heard of again.

In addition to the disasters, resulting from storms, are those caused by fire, collisions, explosions, piracy and the carnage of war. O, how many precious lives have found a watery grave; how much human blood has mingled with the briny waters of the deep.

> "The sea 's abyss is one large grave,
> A church-yard is its face;
> A tombstone is each rising wave,
> To mark the burial place."

What hardships and perils are endured by daring mariners and hazarding explorers, has again been illustrated during the recent Greeley expedition to the Arctic regions. Of those twenty-five heroic men, that sailed out of the New York harbor, only six were found by the relief expedition. Seventeen perished of starvation and exposure. One was drowned while hunting seals for food, and one died in the hands of the relieving party after the amputation of a frost-bitten limb. The remaining seven of that brave band were found surrounded by the corpses of a dozen of their companions, and if relief had come to them 48 hours later, they would all have perished. But the moral shipwrecks on life's stormy voyage far outnumber the disasters on the sea.

Besides, they are infinitely more terrible. How many a youth, whom we considered morally staunch, and able to weather the fiercest gale, has suddenly given way before some sudden hurricane of temptation.

His character, once stainless, is sadly defaced. His reputation is gone—and broken hearts cast despairing looks upon the hopeless wreck.

We often speak of the perils of youth. But they are by no means confined to that period of life.

Many a one, who has safely passed through the treacherous breakers, which lie about the harbor of youth, is lost in the open sea of manhood. The saddest moral catastrophes, of which the Bible speaks, occurred in the history of men, who were verging toward the period of old age.

Noah and Lot were far from youth, when they fell before the influence of strong drink; and Demas was not by any means a "novice" when he forsook Paul, "having loved the present world."

David had past the zenith of his life, when he committed the great transgression recorded against him.

And Judas was not an inexperienced youth, but a fully matured man, when he sold his blessed Master for a most contemptible price.

Every period of human life, therefore, is surrounded with danger. The admonition is never untimely—"let him that standeth take heed last he fall."

What a long list of sad moral shipwrecks we might glean from from the inspired page! How many sailed out for heaven in the most gallant style, and yet never reached Beulah land.

Others suffered no complete shipwreck, but entered the destined harbor with broken masts, and rudders gone. Each one of us is called upon to brave the most violent storms. Every day we see some rock, on which men and women, no weaker nor worse than we, are utterly wrecked.

With enthusiastic joy the cry of " land ahead" is greeted after the shortest and most favorable Ocean passage—because all realize what dangers they have escaped. The joy, that must have thrilled the heart of Columbus, when he discovered the dim outlines of a distant coast, surpasses our boldest imagination. But what is this compared with the rapture, that shall fill the Christian's heart, when the detectable mountains shall loom up before him, and he shall cast anchor in the great harbor of the new Jerusalem. There will be no more storms and disasters, but joyful greetings and unalloyed happiness.

Once more, "there will be no more sea," means, there will be *no more mystery.*

All nature is crowded with mystery, but nothing more so, than the Ocean. How little we know of that which lies, and transpires beneath the surface of the waters. No plummet has yet been invented by which the fathomless depths can be sounded. Question upon question arises to our lips as we reflect upon its wonders. How near do the Ocean's caverns run to the central core of the earth. Whence "these inexhaustible supplies of salt which so impregnate its waters, that all the rivers of the earth, pouring into it from the time of creation, have not been able to freshen them?

What constitutes the bed of the Ocean, and with what creatures are these vast realms of waters peopled? "What undescribed monsters, what unimaginable shapes,"—says Dr. Greenwood—"may be moving in the profoundest places of the sea, never seeking, and perhaps never able to seek, the upper waters, and expose themselves to the gaze of man!"

What glittering riches, what heaps of gold, what stores of gems, there must be scattered in lavish profusion in the Ocean's lowest bed! What spoils from all climates, what works of art from all lands have been engulfed by the insatiable and reckless waves! Who shall go down to examine and reclaim this uncounted and idle wealth? Who bears the keys of the deep?

Well might the Psalmist sing—"the sea is his, and he made it." But there are still greater mysteries locked up in the profoundest caves of the Ocean. Thousands upon thousands have found a last resting-place beneath its weltering waves. Where are the bodies of those, who were assigned—like Jonah of old—to its fathomless depths? Who can tell the bereaved the spot to which their affections may cling? It is all mystery.

The Ocean, with its unsolvable problems, is but a striking symbol of human life. What means this brief existence with its tales of pain and sorrow. Why is this useful man, who was a blessing to his family and his country, so suddenly removed by death, while yonder aged man, who has become a burden to himself and others, is spared from year to year. Why is this kind and tenderhearted mother snatched from the large family of little children, while yonder lonely widow, who prays every morn and night "Lord Jesus come quickly," is allowed to tarry. Why should God take away the only child of these prosperous parents, and leave the pauper his half-a-score, who cry with hunger, and shiver with cold? Why should the good suffer with the evil, the new-born babe with its virtue-less mother? There is no end to the whys and wherefores, which rise up day by day in every reflecting mind. Our life is wrapt in mystery. We know but in part, or, as Lord Bacon says—"It is the little, that we know, it is the great that remains unknown." In Heaven, the veil, which hangs over human life, shall be lifted, and we shall know even as we are known. There will be an end of loneliness, sorrow, unrest, insecurity and mystery, because "there will be no more sea." The glories of that world no mortal can portray. "O! what must it be to be there."

My brother, is your frail bark bound for that blessed port? Is every tempest bringing you nearer to that eternal harbor? Is the Galilean Pilot standing at your helm? Have you given yourself entirely up to him, for time and eternity? Have you asked him to conduct you safely to land? If he is aboard, there is no danger, no matter how the winds may howl and the ocean may roar. He ruleth the winds and the waves. His "peace, be still," produces a great calm, which is but a prelude and prophecy of that blissful felicity which awaits us on that sinless soil.

In the darkest and dreariest hours of life, let your soul be stayed on him. Then you can cheerfully sing:

> "Thus my heart the hope will cherish,
> While to Thee I lift mine eye;
> Thou wilt save me ere I perish,
> Thou wilt hear the sailor's cry,
> And though mast and sail be riven,
> Soon life's voyage will be o'er;
> Safely moored in Heaven's wide haven,
> Storms and tempest vex no more."

The Lord Risen.

———:———

The Lord is risen indeed, and hath appeared to Simon.   Luke 24:34.

AMONG the ten different manifestations of our Lord after his resurrection, this one to Peter is by no means the least important.

We know the history of this ⁎disciple. He belonged to the more inner circle of the Master's disciples; to that favored three, who were eye and ear-witnesses of the greatest events of his life. Peter was naturally brave and fearless, but quite impetuous.

His heart beat warmly for the Master, for whose sake he had cheerfully exchanged a few years ago his employment of a fisher of the deep for a fisher of men.

When his Lord was passing under the dark cloud of his approaching end, and ominous words fell from his lips, he repeatedly expressed his ardent, heart-felt love for him. And when he foretold him, in the clearest language, that he would deny him, and prove unfaithful, he exclaimed in the zeal of his enthusiasm "Though all men shall be offended because of thee, yet will I never be offended." Poor Simon! How little he realized his weakness, and the fiery temptations, which were before him.

Scarcely a few hours had elapsed after these strong assertions, when he denied his Master with the most horrible oaths, and imprecations, and at that sorrowful and reminding look of Jesus, he goes out and weeps bitterly.

God alone, who reads human hearts, as we do countenances, knows what transpired in the breast of this fallen apostle.

How deeply he deplored his sin, and how severely he denounced the pride and self-confidence of his heart, which brought him to this depth of spiritual woe. O, what words of self-condemnation, and sharp rebuke fell from his lips, as he roamed in solitude, along the shores of the Galilean Sea, hiding his face in the ample folds of his mantle. Yes, no artist can portray, nor poet justly describe, the mental anguish and inward grief of this broken-hearted man.

O, how much he thought of Jesus! What precious years those had been which he spent in his fellowship. What debt of love he owed him for his matchless teachings, for his affection and confidence in him. How kindly he had dealt with him. Had he not foreseen his fall? Had he not repeatedly warned him?

O, how could he be thus unfaithful to such a friend in this dark hour of his life. Will he now fall in the hands of his enimies and be removed from him by death? Shall he never see his face again; never hear his pardoning word? But has he not said, when he predicted his fall, " I have prayed for thee that thy faith fail not," "and when thou art converted, strengthen thy brethren?" Thoughts like these no doubt filled the busy brain of this penitent disciple. Rightly has it been remarked, "there is a peculiar silence in the narrative about Peter through all the remaining passion of Christ. He does not appear in the story when he was laid in Joseph's tomb; and nothing is said of him during the three days of great "suspense endured by all the believers at Jerusalem." These three days had doubtless been spent by him in solitude and prayer. O, how long they must have seemed to him. What a period of suspense this was. How pale his cheeks have grown. No wonder, for his "tears have been his meat day and night." But a brighter day has dawned on the horizon, a brighter day for all, and especially for Peter. At the faint streak of dawn, the noble, devoted women, who had lingered latest by the cross, went with sad and timid steps to the sepulcher, where the greatest treasure of their heart lay buried. As they are on their way to the grave, difficulties, of which they had not previously thought, arise before their minds. "Who should roll away for them the great stone, which closed the sepulcher?"

This thought is enough to discourage them completely, and to induce them to return. But they, who could stand at the foot of the cross to the last, do not allow themselves so easily to be moved from their purpose.

They press on in spite of difficulties, and who can describe their astonishment, when they find no guard nor stone to hinder them, but an empty tomb? As they look with mute astonishment into the deserted tomb, angels appear to them, who assure them that the Lord they seek is risen. Soon the Lord himself meets their wondering eyes, and commands them to carry this information of his resurrection to his disciples, and to tell them, that he would go before them, like a shepherd, into their own beloved and native Galilee.—They are, moreover, to bear a special message to Peter. The great shepherd, who laid down his life for his flock, had especially thought of this wandering sheep. He must have a separate message of what has transpired on this memorable morn. O, how much of love these words bespeak— "*tell Peter!*"

When these women, in a tumult of rapture and alarm, have conveyed these messages to the apostles, they do not believe them, but look upon them as idle tales of weak and excitable women. But soon Mary of Magdala comes, who has received a separate and special intimation. Peter and John now determine to go and see for themselves. They find the grave in the condition as described by the women, and here first dawned upon them the trembling hope, that the Savior might have arisen. That very day, where or at what hour we know what, Peter was favored with that manifestation, of which our text speaks, and which has doubtless added no little to that overwhelming conviction, which characterized all his public addresses, and was the cause of his marvellous success as an apostolic preacher. He knew of the things whereof he testified. He was as sure of Christ's resurrection, as of his own personal existence. Or is it possible, that the apostle Peter was a *false* witness, for *such* he must have been, unless he thoroughly knew the things concerning which he testified.

Have you ever seen a brave and fearless man, such as Peter was, who was an habitual liar? We ask not whether, in moments of fearfulness, he may not have been tempted to speak untruthfully, but will this be the even tenor of his day?

Will he not step aside to weep bitterly, and after that cling more firmly to the right than ever? Such we know was Peter's course. Christianity, aside from Paul, has never had a more positive and daring advocate.—Without the slightest embarrassment, this rude Galilean appeared before the kings and councils of the world, protesting, that he *knew* that the Lord was risen. How shall we account for this fact? Rightly asks the celebrated Robertson—"can we believe that the man, who laid his hand on the axe's sharp edge, or he, who asked that he might be crucified with his head downwards, as unworthy to die as his Redeemer died—can we believe that *he* went through all his life falsely? that his life was not only a falsehood, but a systematic and continued falsehood, kept up to the very last; and that the bravehearted, true man, with his dying lips, gave utterance to a lie?"

It is the height of folly to assert that this firm, abiding belief in the resurrection, for which Peter surrendered his life, was the result of an excited imagination. Who ever heard anything like this? You might as well maintain that hunger can produce bread, or the longing of the eye for sunlight arrest its course in the heavens, as to affirm, that the desire for Christ's resurrection could lead the apostles from their condition of doubt, to that of absolute certainty.—There are some incidental facts connected with the story of Christ's resurrection, which must have considerable weight with every unbiased reader of the New Testament. Take this narrative of our Lord's appearance to Peter.

If this composition of this history had been the work of fiction, this incident would not have been communicated to us in so few words and so indirectly. It would have received considerable space, and would have been ornamented no little. For what chance there is here for a vivid imagination to expand, and to furnish a story upon which the imaginative mind would feast with intense delight? Yes, even we, who accept the Bible, as an all-sufficient, divine revelation, would like to have known a little more about this touching manifestation of our Lord to Peter. Still the thought, that this book is not given us as a means to gratify our insatiable curiosity, but as a book to furnish us with facts necessary to the establishment of our hearts in the faith, leads us to adore the wonderful wisdom of God.

Another strong presumptive evidence, which we discern here in favor of the resurrection story, is the *striking agreement* which we observe between Jesus' character *before* and *after* his resurrection, as sketched by these Evangelists. When we think of Peter's condition, at this time, and then read, that the Lord appeared unto *him*, we involuntarily exclaim, "that is just like him!"

We have in the statement of this fact, a *touching proof of Christ's unchangeable love*. Who needed a visit from the risen Savior so much as Peter? What sad hours had he spent! No one could dry those thickly falling tears, and bind up his spirit, save the Master, whom he had so grievously denied. Jesus realized his need of him, and so he favored him with his appearance, before any of the other apostles.

He desires to assure all of his return from the realm of death, and to shed abroad in their sorrowing hearts a joy, such as earth cannot afford.

But Peter has the preference. His eyes shall behold the Lord before any of his brethren. He shall catch the first accents from his lips. His heart shall be filled with music, while others are still mourning.

Thomas, James, even John, who has been faithful to the last, can wait, but this pitiable one needs first of all the soul's physician. No one of the eleven—for one is no more—lies so closely at the divine heart of Jesus, at this time, as this penitent disciple, who amid a flood of tears had rushed forth from the palace of Caiaphas into the night. As the mother who has lost a child, and has still another, who is an invalid, hovers and yearns over this one, more than over all the rest of her family, so does our Savior with his spiritually ailing apostle. Who does not here recall the language of the Psalmist, "Like as a father pitieth his children, so the Lord pitieth them that fear him;" or the Lord's own touching parable of the lost sheep.

Another thing which is remarkable here is the fact, that Jesus appeared to Simon in *solitude*. He prepares him, however, for his coming. He does not rush upon him unexpectedly. This would have frightened this disciple, smitten with guilt, beyond measure. But he has previously prepared him for this appearance, by that consoling message entrusted to the women—"tell Peter."

From this he has learned, that his Master has not forgotten, but is still kindly disposed towards him. What transpired between Jesus and Peter, angels alone have witnessed. It was very proper, that this first interview between our Lord and the disciple, who had denied him, should be strictly private. Words of rebuke and admonition, as well as words of love and pardon, were no doubt here administered. If this had been done publicly, it might have proved a damage to Simon, and his fellow companions might ever after this have looked upon their fallen brother, as greatly inferior to themselves. Although we may not presume to know in what manner Peter's tears are dried, and what the nature of this revelation was, one thing however is certain, that it was more than a *fugitive* vision. Would this have stopped his bleeding heart? Would this have turned his mourning into dancing; have put off his sackcloth, and girded him with gladness?"

We observe further that this appearance of the Lord to Peter *was of incalculable benefit to him.*

Who can tell how dark and stormy it had been within his soul after that black crime which he committed. What painful self-condemnation, what inexplicable doubts, what bitter regrets filled his mind, and made these three days the saddest portion of his life. It is true, he was kept from sinking into the midnight of remorse and of despair. As has been so beautifully expressed by Canon Farrar "if the angel of Innocence had left him, the angel of Repentance took him gently by the hand."

Still there is no doubt, but that the prince of darkness repeatedly aimed his arrows at him, and made him the object of his frequent attacks. He ceased not to sift him as the wheat, until the Lord appeared.—Then light broke in upon the darkness of his soul. Then he knew that the Lord still loved him, and that he still considered him as one of his friends. Then, too, the burden of his guilt, beneath which he had groaned and staggered during these past days, dropped from his shoulders, and with a light heart he pursued his earthly career, accepting at his Master's hand sweet or bitter, whatever he might see fit to bestow. No one of the apostolic circle was happier on the evening of the third day than Peter. Never can he forget that hour, when the risen Savior manifested to him his condescending grace, and sent him off on his way rejoicing. When he afterwards thought of it, he must have been constrained to exclaim in grateful tribute to his Redeemer "thy gentleness hath made me great." Truly he had been gentle with him, "as a nurse cherisheth her children?"

This appearance of the Lord to Simon, *was a source of joy to all the disciples*, but it must have been especially a source of surprise to the brethren from Emmaus, who came even at this late hour of day to tell, that they had talked and travelled and dined with him. But before they have a chance to communicate their experience, the Jerusalem brethren exclaim to them in exultation, "the Lord is risen indeed, and hath appeared to Simon."

One great benefit, which might accrue to them from this manifestation to Peter, was this, that it determined their demeanor with reference to him. They must henceforth look upon him, not as one whom the Lord had rejected, but as one upon whom he had bestowed his highest favor. We cannot sufficiently admire the *wisdom*, as well as the love, of our Redeemer in this entire transaction.

If he had not revealed himself to Peter, we can see how natural it would have been for them to consider him as quite inferior to themselves. Yes, it might have led them to exclude him, like another Judas, from their circle. It is true, the Lord had formerly spoken very gracious words to him, and had apparently exalted him above the rest of them. But were not these eminent favors the result of that splendid confession, "thou are the Christ, the Son of the living God?" They might, therefore, have reasoned thus, that as these privileges were conferred upon him, as the result of his bold and resolute confession, that he had now forfeited them on account of his disgraceful cowardice.

Who can tell with what distrustful eye they might hereafter have looked upon him, and inquired of themselves whether behind all this external devotion lay not concealed a traitor's heart. Jesus, therefore, understanding human nature better than the best of us, revealed himself to Peter first, in some secluded spot, where he could tell him all. The Lord, who only is just and gracious, knew all the circumstances in Simon's case. He saw that it had been no wilful and permanent abandonment of his Christian profession, but a temporary unfaithfulness owing to the weakness of his flesh. Even behind the awful oaths and curses, which fell from his lips, he had detected a heart of love.

He fathomed the depth of his present distress, and therefore carried to him that Easter-benediction, which presently all shall receive—"peace be unto you."

The apostles received from Peter's lips the first assurances of Christ's resurrection. The assertions of the women they look upon as idle tales, and the sight of the empty tomb, and the dispersed watch merely awaken the thought of a bare possibility. But when Simon tells what he has heard and seen, their despondency is turned into joy, and their doubts into expectancy, and they enthusiastically exclaim—"the Lord is risen indeed."

That fact, that Peter had seen the risen Savior, before any of them, was an unmistakable proof of Christ's abiding love for him, and was all-sufficient to restore him to the esteem and fellowship of the remaining ten. If Jesus had so lovingly forgiven him, who were they, that they should harbor a grudge against him. If he was still dear to the Master, why not to them? This excellent apostle may never be able to forgive himself, and may in his writings indirectly refer to his sad fall, and on that account so frequently sound the note of alarm, his fellow associates never speak discreditably of him, but cover his weakness with the mantle of Christian charity.

To be sure, when they come to give us a history of Jesus' life, they do not overlook Peter's fall, without which these Gospels would be quite incomplete. But they at the same time definitely show how fully this wanderer was restored to them, as well as to his Master. If "all scripture is given by inspiration, and is profitable for doctrine, for reproof, for correction, for instruction in righteousness, that the man of God may be perfect, thoroughly furnished unto all good works"–if this be the grand aim of every part of the divine Word, then it has no doubt pleased the Holy Spirit to preserve the incident, upon which we have dwelt, for our spiritual good. We may therefore glean some important practical suggestions from the information here given.

It seems to me that we have here, first of all, an *incentive to faith*. O how faithless and unbelieving we frequently are. We are so inclined to measure our Savior by ourselves. How little the most advanced Christian among us knows of that love, which passeth knowledge, and whose height and depth and length and breadth no creature can compute. Can we have a more touching exhibition of Jesus' love, than we have here? Peter, who had so vilely violated the obligations of friendship, but who was truly penitent, was not forgotten by his Lord. Could anything prove more conclusively that he was really the Chief Shepherd of the sheep, who had brought back with him from the dead the faithful shepherd-heart?

Truly, he is the LORD in all the force of the word; the Lord of each of his followers, of his whole Church, of heaven and earth together. He cherished a most tender love for the lost and wandering. He himself goes after the lost sheep in the wilderness, and brings it home upon his shoulders with great rejoicing. Let every poor fallen disciple, therefore, look to him in full assurance of faith. Like Peter, you may have been grievously unfaithful. Your sin may be like mountains, but his mercy reacheth unto the heavens. He looks after you first of all. Remember what he has said—"they that are whole need not a physician, but they that are sick."

Again, we have here a *powerful incentive to love*. If Jesus is so kindly disposed towards those, who have departed from the path of rectitude, if he cannot bear to leave them to their disconsolate condition, but gives them the warmest tokens of his love and sympathy, who are we, that we should withdraw ourselves, or abuse with our harsh language the penitent Simon for whom

Jesus died. O my friends, how little we have of our Lord's loving spirit. How frequently is he compelled to rebuke us, and to say—"Ye know not what manner of spirit ye are of." Certainly, we are not of Christ's spirit, when we chide the fallen Peters, and say "well, it is your own fault, you were warned, you ought to have been more watchful, and less self-confident." This may be all true, but it is not the proper way to speak, when one's heart is already crushed with sorrow. Let us therefore seek to possess the mind of Christ, and listen to Paul's Christ-like exhortation—" Brethren, if a man be overtaken in a fault, ye, who are spiritual, restore such a one in the spirit of meekness, considering thyself, lest thou also be tempted."

Lastly, we have here an incentive to *hope*. It is no wonder, that Peter after his thrice-repeated denial, went out and wept bitterly. When he looked at his sin and all its aggravations, we are not at all surprised, that the sky of his soul was wrapt in deepest gloom. But the grace of God, like a bow of promise, spanned these ominous clouds. "Sternly, yet tenderly, the spirit of grace—says a certain divine, "led up this broken-hearted penitent before the tribunal of his own conscience, and there his old life, his old shame, his old weakness, his old self, was doomed to that death of godly sorrow, which was to issue in a new and nobler birth."

What a difference between his sorrow, and that of Judas, in its nature as well as in its results. The reason was, that he still clung to God's mercy. His hope never forsook him. When we look at the Great Physician's treatment of this spiritual patient, hope must revive in every breast troubled by sin. Say not "my sin is too great to be pardoned." "I have wandered away so far, and have gone into such devious paths, that it does not seem to me as if Christ could forgive me, and receive me back to his fold." O my friend, you know not how wonderful he is in long-suffering, and how infinite in loving-kindness.

All that he asks of you is a cordial acknowledgement, and a deep, genuine sorrow for sin.

Does it grieve you, that you have offended your best of friends so shamefully and persistently? Do you desire to live, wholly consecrated to him? Can you say, even in view of your manifold backslidings—"Lord, thou knowest all things, thou knowest that I love thee?" Then take courage, no matter what darts satan may send in your soul, and with what anxiety your restless heart may beat—the Lord will cause light to arise out of darkness. Only see to it, that your sorrow be of the right kind—that "godly sorrow, which worketh repentance unto salvation, not to be repented of."

While the Lord manifested himself to the broken-hearted Simon, he passed by the prejudiced and hard-hearted Annas and Caiaphas. He only revealed himself to those, who were truly ready to receive him.

Are we, my friends, ready to receive the bright and ever brightening manifestations of the Son of God in our hearts? Or do we still lack the humble heart of Simon, which so earnestly craved salvation. The sightless eye cannot behold the glories of the sun, nor the heart which is filled, enjoy the bounties of that spiritual banquet, which God has prepared for every needy child of his. If we only have susceptible hearts, we may have a peace and joy akin to that of the apostles in the upper chamber at the close of this Easter day. But without this, even heaven must be a lonesome and dreary place.

Let us, therefore, above all earthly attainments, seek to acquire that true disposition of heart, in which God delights, and which prepares us for the splendors of a world which never ends.

Preached on morning of last Sabbath of author's life--day before he died. Therefore requested.

Jehovah's Tender Care.

> As an eagle stirreth up her nest, fluttereth over her young, spreadeth abroad her wings, taketh them, beareth them on her wings, so the Lord alone did lead him, and there was no strange god with him. Deut. 32,11-12.

GOD'S dealings with Israel form a most remarkable and interesting page in the world's history. He was their Leader.

But his divine leadership is not confined to his old covenant people. "The Lord is a great King over all the earth." "The philosophy of history," of which scholars speak, is but another name for Providence. The forces of society are the wisdom and power of a personal God.

Benjamin Franklin said in Congress "I have lived, sir, a long time; and the longer I live, the more convincing proof I see of this truth, that God governs the affairs of men."

Our illustrious American sage and statesman only echoed the sentiments, which some eighteen hundred years ago fell from the lips of the celebrated Cicero, who said "what can be so thoroughly plain, as that there is some divinity, by whom these things are governed?" It is human ignorance alone, which confounds the infinite with the finite, that sweeps an omnipotent ruler from the throne of the Universe. Why should it be thought a thing incredible, that an infinite God, who has set a million of worlds revolving in space, should watch with sleepless interest over the life of the feeblest of his creatures on this little planet of ours? What burden can such a government be to him, whose mind is illimitable, and whose power is without exhaustion? "Hast thou not known? hast thou not heard, that the everlasting God, the Lord, the Creator of the ends of the earth, fainteth not, neither is weary? there is no searching of his understanding." Those sublime truths of God's Sovereignty, and the universality of his reign, which beamed upon intelligent minds during the darkest periods of the world's history, form a part of the most positive declarations of Holy Writ. Here we are taught, that God not only holds the stars in their courses, and the Ocean in the hollow of his hand, but that he directs the steps of man, yea the flight of an insignificant sparrow, and numbers the very hairs of our heads. In the dreariest hours of life, the believing soul cheerfully sings:

"In each event of life how clear
Thy ruling hand I see,
Each blessing to my heart more dear,
Because conferred by thee."

Of course, this fact does not do away with the widest scope of human freedom. All about us we see men acting out their plans and designs with the greatest possible freedom, as if there came no voice from the throne saying—"my counsel shall stand, I will do all my pleasure." Much happens in the government of God, which is done merely permissively, and would never transpire, if men were in perfect harmony with their Creator's will.

But notwithstanding all this, he infallibly controls and overrules human acts and purposes, and makes them subservient to a most glorious end. In the text, Moses is rehearsing in song God's miraculous guidance of his people. Amid the glittering wealth of eloquence, that burst from the grateful heart of the aged prophet, we find the beautiful comparison of the text, borrowed from natural history.

Using the lesser to illustrate the greater, he compares God's dealings with his chosen people to the treatment of the mother eagle with her young. This king of birds, which builds its nest on a mountain top in the clefts of the rocks, is noted for its strong attachment to its offspring, and is the subject of frequent allusion in Scripture. We are here made acquainted with the manner in which it deals with its young, which furnishes illustrations of the most comforting spiritual truths.

1. The first thought, which we have presented here, is this, that DISCIPLINE IS A NECESSARY ELEMENT IN THE SPIRITUAL EDUCATION OF GOD'S PEOPLE.

For many weeks, the mother bird has tenderly fed her young, and brought them fresh provisions every hour. She has marked their growth. Their baldness is gone. They are covered all over with feathers. Their wings are maturing, but for want of exercise are still weak and powerless. She knows that tf they shall answer their destiny, and cleave the skies with their wings, and mount up to the sun, they most get away from the old nest to which they are so strongly attached. As often as she returns from her flight, she finds them still clinging to the nest, dozing and blinking. In this condition their powers of flight will never be developed. In various ways she tries to get them on the wing But all is in vain. So she resorts to more effectual means. She puts her claws deep in the nest, shakes it up, turns the inside out, makes it perfectly uncomfortable for them. How cruel this maternal instinct seems. How pitiful these young eagles scream out their distress. Could they speak, with what severity they would reprove the unkindness of their mother.

They would say, " what wrong have we been guilty of, that we thus should be broken up and cast out upon the cold world?" What an apt illustration is this of God's conduct toward his people. Turn to the pages of sacred and ecclesiastical history, and you will read on almost every page of the stirring up of the nest.

The children of Israel would never have wished to leave the brick-ovens of Egypt, and would not have put forth the slightest efforts to obtain possession of the land promised to their illustrious ancester, if the Lord had not stirred up their nest.

But another ruler ascended to the throne of Egypt, who knew not Joseph. The lives of Jacob's sons were embittered by cruel bondage.

Their burdens were made intolerable. They dragged out a miserable existence. Their daughters were for slaves, and their sons for slaughter. O how they screamed, and were frightened, when the old nest was stirred up beneath them. But see, what a glorious purpose it served. Look at this people after the lapse of a century or more. See them during the golden period of David and Solomon. Who would have thought, that these degraded slaves could ever have developed into such a prosperous nation, which has poured lustre on the scroll of history. Follow this people in their course down the stream of time. Jeshurun waxed fat and kicked. Prosperity became their downfall. They began to forget the Lord, whose powerful arm had led them all the way. They entered into alliance with foreign nations. They introduced strange gods among them. They erected altars in honor to them on every high mountain, and their abominations filled the land.

The rod of divine displeasure must be applied, or they will perish in their sin. See how their comfortable nest is torn to pieces, as the armies of Babylon are sent among them to devastate their country, and to carry away the flower of their land into captivity.

For seventy years, their plundered land presented a scene of total desolation; and when at length they were permitted to rebuild its waste places, the salutary effects of their temporary bondage had stamped itself upon their national life.

Never were a people more effectually cured of their degradations, than the children of Israel of their idolatry. Whatever sin they committed after their captivity, there were no more strange gods among them.

2. This truth of the text WE SEE ALSO ILLUSTRATED IN THE EARLY CHRISTIAN CHURCH. The saints at Jerusalem after pentecost were greatly prosperous and were walking together in the joys and comforts of the Gospel.

Like the disciples on Mount Tabor, in the presence of their transfigured Master, they felt like rearing tabernacles, and exclaimed in their joy—" it is good for us to be here!"

If the hand of the Lord had not interfered, Christianity would have crystallized into a mere local institution. But the persecution, which arose at the time of Stephen's death, scattered the disciples in every direction, and in a short time these scattered fire-brands had set the whole Roman Empire ablaze.

Repeatedly the saying has been verified in the history of the Christian Church, that "truth, like a torch, the more it's shook it shines."

As in nature, the very fierceness of the storm carries the arrowy seed from the parent stem on its downy wings to a kindlier and more fertile soil, so the most bitter opposition to the cause of Christ, has given it a fresh impulse and a larger sphere of usefulness.

When we come down to modern times, we see the truth of our text vividly illustrated in the history of our puritan fathers. After the most bloody persecutions the Protestants rejoiced when Queen Elizabeth, herself a Protestant, ascended the throne. They looked for a reign of religious prosperity. But alas! how quickly the sharp claw of religious intolerance tore their quiet nest into fragments. For fifty long years they were persecuted without cessation. The caves and dens of the earth became their sanctuaries. Hundreds of puritan ministers were reduced to poverty, and were subject to all manner of mal-treatment. Many of these heroic men quit their native land, and crossed over to Holland, until finally we find them on this side of the Atlantic actively engaged in laying the broad and deep foundations of this glorious republic. If these early colonists, by the stirring of their peaceful nest, had not been thrown upon their own resources, we might not, to this day, have enjoyed the blessings of civil and religious liberty.

The finger of God is distinctly seen in all the periods of our past history. If England had been a little more just and merciful, we might, to this day, have been one of its most loyal and prosperous tributaries.

Had not the hand of traitors insulted the stars and stripes, that waved on Bunker Hill, the clanking of the chains of millions of bondmen would still be ringing in our ears, and the withering curse of slavery would still retard the moral and religious progress of this mighty nation. What we are to-day, we owe to that mysterious providence, which did not according to our mind, but according to its own infinite wisdom. It was the stirring of the nest that brought us on the wing, and led us to soar above clouds and tempest........

The truth of our text we see also illustrated in the lives of *individual Christians.*

There is no truly great man, who has not passed through the

furnace of affliction. They are common, not precious stones, that escape the lapidary's wheel. The vessel, that shines the brightest, has been the most thoroughly scoured. The wild tree may grow in undisturbed repose, but the fruit-bearing orchard tree will bleed at times beneath the pruning knife. The golden law of the kingdom is "whom the Lord loveth, he chasteneth, and he scourgeth every son, whom he receiveth."

Job thought that he would die in his nest. But how unexpectedly it fell away beneath him.

What series of troubles, like a succession of thunder-claps from a clear sky, burst forth over his head. But the sequel showed how much he had gained by this severe trial of his faith. King Manasseh, the son of the good Hezekiah, who, corrupted by wealth and power, trampled upon the godly principles of his early education, would have filled up the measure of his uniquity, had not the Lord stirred up his nest.

But when he was put in fetters and carried away to Babylon, he raised his weeping eyes to heaven, and humbled himself before the God of his fathers. If Nebuchadnezzar had not been brought to the very level of the brute creation, so that he grazed with oxen in the field, and was wet with the dew of heaven, he would never have been cured of his pride and brought to confess, that "the most High God ruled in the kingdom of men, and appointeth over it whomsoever he will."

If the prodigal had not starved by the swine trough, he had never been regaled at his father's table. If Jonah had not been tossed on the tempestuous sea, and spent three days and nights in its mysterious caverns he would never have been the successful preacher he was, who, in a few days, brought an entire wicked city in sack-cloth and ashes before God. If the widow of Zarephath had not looked with horror-stricken eyes on the empty barrel, she would never have welcomed the prophet beneath her roof, who kept her provision from failing.

But why turn to the saints of the past? Are there not many before me this evening, whose Christian experience is described in the words of the Psalmist—"It is good for me that I have been afflicted: before I was afflicted I went astray, but now have I kept thy word."

How many would have continued to lead a prayerless life, if they had not met with the most serious reverses, and learned through personal experience, that he "builds too low, who builds beneath the skies."

Some would never have been rich in heavenly possessions, if their earthly treasures had not taken wings and fled away. Some would never have laid hold of that hope, "which is an anchor to the soul, both sure and steadfast," if their earthly hopes had not been completely frustrated. If you had not been standing by the ashes of your earthly Ziklags, you would not have learned to look so intently for "the city, which hath foundations, whose builder and maker is God." If the prospects of your earthly Canaan had not faded from your view, you would not have been so ready to prepare for the Heavenly Canaan. When the rose of health faded from your cheeks, and your couch of suffering was wet with tears, you turned your haggard face to the wall, like the pious Hezekiah, and prayed not merely that God might extend your life, but that it might be spent in his service. When you have stooped over the empty cradle, and missed the carols of a sweet-voiced family bird, you thought of Jesus' words—"of such is the kingdom of heaven," and your stubborn knees were almost unconsciously bent in prayer, and your hardened heart grew wonderfully tender.

O, what family nest does not feel these divine disturbances! I care not upon what mountain-top or in what lofty cedar it is built, and how secure and inaccessible to danger it may seem. In an unexpected hour, we are driven out of it, and all seems desolate about us. Happy are we, if these experiences lead us to sing:

> "Now to the shining realms above,
> I stretch my hands, and glance mine eyes,
> Oh for the pinions of a dove,
> To bear me to the upper skies!
>
> There, from the bosom of my God,
> Oceans of endless pleasure roll:
> There would I fix my last abode,
> And drown the sorrows of my soul."

3. But the text does not only call attention to the discipline connected with God's leadership, it also points out HIS INSTRUC-

TION BOTH BY PRECEPT AND EXAMPLE. When the old eagle has thoroughly scratched up the nest, she does not abandon her helpless young, but stays nearer them than ever before. She spreads abroad her wings and flutters over them, and so by her own example teaches them to fly. In the same manner does the Lord deal with his children. He is particularly near when the nest is disturbed and our hearts are almost broken with grief, and we know not where to turn or what to do. O how lovingly in such hours he flutters over us, and sets before us a better way of living.

It is a most interesting sight to see the old eagle teach its young the manner of flight. A hunter, who saw two parent eagles instructing two young birds, describes it in the following manner: "They began by rising from the top of the mountain in the eye of the sun. It was about midday and bright for this climate. They at first made small circles and the young birds imitated them. They paused on their wings, waiting till they had made their first flight; and then took a second and larger gyration, always rising towards the sun, and enlarging their circle of flight, so as to make a gradual ascending spiral. The young ones still and slowly followed, apparently flying better as they mounted; and they continued this sublime exercise, always rising, till they became mere points in the air, and the young ones were lost, and afterwards their parents, to our aching sight."

This illustrates but faintly God's marvellous patience in teaching us to soar above this low, grovelling life, which the masses are leading.

How full is this divine book of the most salutary instructions. Here we have line upon line, and precept upon precept. But, better than all this, God has given us a most marvellous example of the highest excellence in the person of his Son.

For thirty-three years, divine goodness walked in human form up and down the land of Palestine. What a grand life that was! It shines like the noonday sun in the firmament of history.

The brightest lives, that men had lived, paled before it, as the stars sink out of sight before the rising orb of day. There is no condition in life which he has not ennobled, no virtue which he has not demonstrated, no human problem upon which he has not poured new light.

He drew men to himself by the infinite attraction of his being. O how he fluttered over sinners and woed them towards Heaven, and wept over Jerusalem, and rejoiced when any repented. By his atoning death and matchless life, he sought to lift men up to fellowship with his Father. That Savior no longer walks among men in visible form, but his life and death are constantly making deeper impressions upon human hearts and lives. He calls upon each one of us to follow him, and to be imitators of him as dear children. All about us we see and hear the flutterings of the divine wings teaching us to soar away to brighter realms. We hear them in the tender messages of love, which Christ's ambassadors bring to us. We see them in the noble examples and transformed lives of God's people around us. My brethren, let us remember that we are Christ's representatives. God teaches men by us, in the family and social relation. By our fruitful lives we must disclose the secret power of truth. Our every day conduct, and not the Bible, is the book which the great mass of people read. Says Pres. Robinson—"You may cover the earth with bibles until it groans beneath the weight of them, and the world is not subdued. The spirit is not in the Bible, but in the living church." We must teach men how to soar above a perishing world, but how can we do this, when we ourselves keep clinging to the old nest, and fold our wings to rest. Let us, in every sphere and relation of life, do all we can to impress men with the beauty and secret power of the religion we profess.

"And as the bird each fond endearment tries,
To tempt her new-fledged offspring to the skies:
Employ each art, reprove each dull delay;
ALLURE to brighter worlds, and LEAD the way."

4. But we have not yet exhausted the beautiful imagery of the text. We read here she "taketh and beareth them on her wings." And again we read "ye have seen how I bare you on eagles' wings." We have a very happy allusion here to the custom of this imperial bird. With inimitable art she entices the young bird to get on her back and then she darts away with it into the air, shakes it off, and when, wing-weary, it begins to sink, she swoops under it again and bears it aloft. What a beautiful illustration this is of the tender love and painstaking of our Heavenly Father. He not merely instructs but assists us. As

the mother holds out her finger to the tottering infant she teaches to walk, so God encourages and assists us in our heavenly course. There are times, when he seems to be severe with us, when he shakes us off, as does the eagle its young; when he makes us deeply conscious of our helplessness when he touches our thigh, as he did Jacob's, in order that in our utter weakness and broken-down condition we may take hold of him with all the firmer grasp, and with all the more intense desire for a blessing.

It may seem cruel to the young bird, when its mother shakes it from her flapping wings in mid-air. But she does this, not that she may dash it to pieces upon the rocks beneath, but that it may learn to rely upon its own resources, and acquire strength to soar heavenward amid the wildest storms.

What the young bird needs is trust in its mother. This is exactly what we need. God's arm is all-powerful. His wings are equal to any emergency. We are safe, if we will only trust him.

There is no duty in which he will not help and support us. He sends us no trial, but what he gives strength to bear it. When he calls us to scale rugged mountains, he equips us with shoes of iron and brass. When he calls us to pass through roaring seas, he cleaves the swelling waves, and leads us through dry-shod; and when his people are cast into the fiery oven of affliction, he walks with them amid its crackling flames. When Paul felt the excruciating pain of his thorn in the flesh, and was ready to sink, God puts his wings under him saying "my grace is sufficient for thee."

But while God will *protect* and *support* his children, he expects them to do their part. He never encourages neglect or cowardice. When Jesus wrought his marvellous cures among the people of Judea and Galilee, he illustrated the truth, that God helps those, who help themselves—"Stretch forth the withered hand" —"Arise take up thy bed and walk," such were the commands which constantly fell from his lips. That does not mean, that any real strength or virtue can proceed from us; but it does mean, that we are held responsible for the obedient use of whatever natural or spiritual strength we possess, as God may confer.

Let us go forth trusting in him, who multiplieth strength to them that have no power. To the Christian the belief of the Red

Indian, who maintains that the strength of every defeated and scalped enemy passes into his conqueror's arms, is true in a loftier, grander sense.

He who cannot lie, has spoken, "As thy days, so shall thy strength be."

"They that wait upon the Lord shall renew their strength; they shall mount up with wings as eagles; they shall run and not be weary, and they shall walk and not faint."

O what glorious possibilities lie before the child of God! "It doth not yet appear what we shall be." The human mind can not conceive of the fresh vigor and increasing glory, that the growing millenniums shall add to our immortal life. Here the unresting beat of the waves of the sea of time gnaws away the bank and shoal whereon we stand; but there each roll of that great Ocean of eternity shall but spread new treasures at our feet and add new acres to our immortal heritage.

My brethren, let us not grow discouraged then, when the Lord shakes up the nest in which you had been so comfortably resting. Realize that you need this overturning in order to loosen your too strong attachment to the material and perishable, and to be brought on the wing to a nobler clime, and more enduring possessions. Let your eye be ever fixed on the Savior, who hovers about you and trains you for the noblest flights. Let the last word of a dying saint be the motto of your life, "higher," "higher."

> "Upward where the stars are burning,
> Silent, silent, in their turning,
>   Round the never-changing pole;
> Upward where the sky is brightest,
> Upward where the blue is lightest,
>   Lift I now my longing soul.
> Far above that arch of gladness,
> Far beyond these clouds of sadness,
>   Are the many mansions fair.
> Far from pain and sin and folly,
> In that palace of the holy,—
>   I would find my mansion there.
> Where the glory brightly dwelleth,
> Where the new song sweetly swelleth,
>   And the discord never comes;
> Where life's stream is ever laving,
> And the palm is ever waving,
>   That must be the home of homes."

This sermon preached on the evening before the author's death and therefore the last he ever preached.

www.ingramcontent.com/pod-product-compliance
Lightning Source LLC
Chambersburg PA
CBHW020310170426
43202CB00008B/567